WORLD RELIGION AND MODERN ART

By Anthony Padgett
M.A., P.G.C.E.

2

Published by
The Auditors of God

First Published 2011
Copyright Anthony Padgett 2011

ISBN 978-0-9561587-9-6

WORLD RELIGION AND MODERN ART

Dedicated to
Stephanie Sturges
Mum & Dad

Cover Picture: "Prophet of Postmodern Art" - 2004
Enamel On Digital Print Canvas 50 x 80cm, Anthony Padgett.

TABLE OF CONTENTS

PREFACE

From 1994 – 2005 I investigated the relationship between art and religion. These complex issues never got interest from people in an art-world that was anti-religious and a religious world that remained within narrow doctrinal viewpoints. Both groups had fixed views concerning what is religious and what is artistic.

Between 2005 and 2008 I conducted an extensive Employment Tribunal case against the Tate Galleries, London, over issues of institutional religious discrimination in the art world. I successfully defended myself against numerous attempts to throw the case out on technicalities and the case was only thrown out at the Court of Appeal on the grounds that it concerned a submission for exhibiting artwork rather than a performance (despite my application stating clearly it was for a performance) I had already given up on believing there was any accountability or fairness in the art-world, now I had also lost my naïve faith in the judicial system. I felt that I would give up creating art. However, I was inspired to write a novel about religion and art, called "The Rainbow Swastika Conspiracy". And this was my final artwork and led to my creating a Register of Originality for artists.

At the end of 2010 I visited a conference on Spirituality, Religion and Contemporary Art. Shocked by how little development had still occurred in the field I decided to write this short introduction to some of the issues. The following draws out some of the key points involved in the complex relationship between art and religion and makes the connections between them as easy to understand as is possible.

Anthony Padgett 2011

BIOGRAPHY

Anthony Padgett has a BA in Philosophy, a PGDip in Conservation of Stonemasonry, a PGCE in the Teaching of Religious Education, and an MA in the Theory of Contemporary Art and Performance.

From 1995 -1999 he worked with the British School of Archaeology in Jerusalem, the Israeli Antiquities Authority, the Palestinian Department of Antiquities, Lancaster University Archaeological Unit and the Historic American Buildings Survey, Washington D.C.

From 1999-2005 his art was in numerous group and solo exhibitions, and he was an Artist-in-Residence at Loughborough University, the winner of the About Vision Art & Technology Award (London), a finalist in the International Jewish Artist of the Year Award 2004, an A-foundation commissioned artist for Liverpool Biennial 2004 and a performer at Edinburgh Fringe 2005.

His work includes an award winning sculpture "Zoroastrian Icarus", art experiments in Jerusalem on Millennium Eve, performance art and his 2 year Employment Tribunal case against Mr Tony Blair and the Trustees of the Tate Gallery. His final artwork was "The Rainbow Swastika Conspiracy" - a book based on his experiences and on prophecies about financial corruption and global conflict.

His work has been featured in the Guardian, the Mail on Sunday, Times Online, Times Educational Supplement and BBC Radio 4. He has given talks about contemporary religious art at various venues, including the New York Studio School of Art, the Institute of Contemporary Art and Tate Modern.

"And birth they do not use
Nor death on Betelgeuse,
And the God, of whom we are
Infinite dust, is there
A single leaf of those
gold leaves on Betelgeuse."

The last verse of "Betelgeuse" 1925, Humbert Wolfe (1886-1940)
Poet, civil servant and great, great uncle of the author.

INTRODUCTION

The difficulty in a study of Religions and Modern Art is that people tend to have quite strong personal opinions about both. This restricts what they are prepared to look at in terms of religions and in terms of art.

Another difficulty is that the subject is so broad that it is very difficult for people to get an overview. They feel at sea and so they restrict their interests and studies to specific areas that they identify with.

For the purposes of the book, I would like to ask you to open your mind up to a broad range of religions of the world and also a broad range of art forms and styles. Only then will we be able to make an analysis that can look to the heart of what constitutes religion and art and thus to the heart of what constitutes religious art. This is not an exhaustive study of religion and art but charts some of the main areas.

The book is called "World Religion And Modern Art" (rather than World Religions) because it reflects the people in the Artworld's unconscious desire to create a global religious viewpoint through Modern Art.

There are many artists whose works would be interesting to look at but to restrict this book to a manageable proportion I have just dealt with some typical examples. This nonetheless includes the work of over 100 artists.

WORLD RELIGION

14

DEFINITIONS OF RELIGIOUS TERMS

There are 5 main areas that we need to look at in relation to religion. These are Religion, Morality, Spirituality, Mysticism and the Divine.

Religion – this is broadly characterised as the faith in God(s) or external supernatural power or powers that are intelligent. And to have faith alone does not make you religious as atheism is a form of faith.

The term religion is associated with the physical, incarnated forms of Gods and with stories of their actions. Believers can have revelations and visions. It is also concerned with rituals, doctrines, sacrifice, theology, ceremony, acts of worship and the priestly institutions and organisations.

Religion is often defined as requiring a large following eg Christianity and Islam, with smaller or more recent groups being called "cults", "sects" and "new religious movements" e.g. Scientology and Sufism. We will look at both belief systems that are called religions and ones that are called cults because religious artistic expression is often individual, (rather than institutional or widespread). Indeed the artist might even claim to originate their own religion.

Morality – this concerns belief system about what are good and evil actions, and how to follow or avoid them. Some religions argue that morals are created by God(s) and that to be moral require a religious belief. However this creates the circular argument of how did God know which acts to decree as being moral as he needed to see that they were moral or he could have chosen immoral acts. Some atheists argue that religious belief is contrary to morality as it does more harm than good.

Morality contrasts two (dual) positions of good and evil. As such it gives a dualistic point of view. God(s) can be moral (dualistic) or beyond morality (see mysticism below).

Spirituality – the term spirituality is not to be confused with mysticism (a sub-group of spirituality – see below). Spirituality concerns our internal relation to religious powers and forces. It concerns meditation and personal experiences that are often inarticulable. It relates to conscience, desires and to feelings of goodness and peace.

Mysticism – this is the core Enlightenment experience of Hindus, Buddhists, Sufis, Qabbalists and Western Mystics. The reader will find this matter very complicated if they have not experienced mystical consciousness. It is like experiencing a completely new colour. Very few people achieve this state of consciousness and most of those only achieve it briefly. In this mystical experience there are no conceptual oppositions (duality) and so it is called non-dualistic. Everything is interconnected. Even good and evil are ultimately the same and their difference is just an illusion. Nothing is more important than anything else. And even God and humans are of the same essence. In this state of consciousness there is no special meaning or meaninglessness, just an experience of being connected to the fundamental sense of reality that is the same anywhere and at anytime.

The ego of many religious believers leads them to think they have achieved an understanding of mystical consciousness when in reality they are just in a dualistic consciousness that is spiritual. This becomes important later in relation to the understanding and misunderstanding of spiritual art.

Mysticism had a profound influence on the development of religions. A small number of religious people through the ages seek out teachings that express this experience. They connected to other groups of initiated individuals from a variety of religious backgrounds. However, the leaders of the religious tradition that they are from often see mystics as heretical and force them and their teachings underground.

Mysticism can almost be termed Pre-Religious as in some creation myths the mystical state is presented as the original, undivided consciousness that humans had, e.g. a Judaeo-Christian Eden like state, before sin when mankind became self-conscious and divided (dualism).

The moral consciousness is distinct from the mystical consciousness but there is some common ground between them as those who experience the states have some continuity of identity between them – although many claim that their true identity is within Enlightenment.

The question of how moral and mystical consciousness relate has been a conundrum for Hindu and Buddhist scholars. Whilst Hindus and Buddhists have consciously struggled with this philosophical issue. I argue that humanity has unconsciously tried to reconcile the two perspectives in art. Before we can see the artistic pattern emerging we need to take an overview on the development of religion and mysticism.

Finally we will use the "Divine" as a term that covers the religious, the spiritual and the mystical. This enables us to speak of these radically different perspectives under a single term.

HISTORY OF RELIGION AND ART

Whilst it is easy to trace the origins of recent religions the origins of the early religions are a source of debate between archaeologists and historians (some of whom have vested interests in the religion of their particular ethnicity or nationality). The following is a brief guide to the features and differences of the world religions that have had the greatest impact on the development of Modern Art.

Our description of religion is tied up with a description of the history of art, as art illustrates ideas in a religion and also charts the influences on the development of a religion.

N.B. - B.C.E. means Before Common Era (replacing B.C.) and C.E. means Common Era (replacing A.D.).

ANIMISM

This prehistoric and tribal religion includes the worship of animals and ancestors. It includes the belief that objects and creatures have a spirit within them and that by connecting with these spirits, through magic rituals, you can influence events. Ritual sacrifices were made and ecstatic, mystical states of altered consciousness were created. The energy from these states was channelled to achieve desired results.

Pre-modern religions were weaved into every aspect of life. They were a way to explain the universe and a way to keep people controlled within a social hierarchy.

The use of art was integral to worship for village communities. Individuals often make images using local materials such as straw, clay, bamboo, stone or cloth. These Icons are used in birth, initiation, marriage and death ceremonies and were part of a visual language that expresses profound concepts and are part of a collective body of mythical beings and symbolic systems. (1)

An example of animism is the original Indian religion (pre-Hindu) of the Dravidians, who worshipped the Nagas, the Snake Gods of the earth, and the spirits living in everything, the trees, rocks, animals, earth and sky.

As humans became more powerful by making tools that separated themselves from their environments and created more complex, hierarchical societies. The psychoanalyst Sigmund Freud thought that religion began with hunting tribes that were dominated by a single male. The male children would fight their father for supremacy and the tribe would eat him if he was defeated and killed. And as humans moved into agriculture they formed societies where fathers were revered as spirits who would help the tribe from the afterlife and were worshipped with statues. These ancestors became animal Gods, who were sacrificed and eaten in fertility rites to promote a good harvest. Freud thought that this was also as a way to control the unconscious instinct to kill the father. In this animism we have the origins of the idea of an older leader i.e. a God/ Messiah/ Father/ King/ Pharaoh, who is sacrificed for the good of the nation.

Humans created Gods as an exaggeration of their own powers. These Gods related to different areas of life and these early religions blended religious, moral, spiritual and mystical elements. However, there was also an underlying belief that these Gods related to aspects of a greater mystical unity.

HINDUISM

Hinduism is the world's oldest living religion, originating from the Indus valley in 3,500 B.C.E. then moving to the Ganges area in 1,900 B.C.E. when the Indus rivers dried up. The Hindu scriptures, the Rig Vedas tell us that Aryan conquerors came, 4,000 years ago, bringing the sky Gods; Agni, the God of Fire, and Indra, the God of Thunder.

But the Dravidians, in India, who worshipped the Earth Mother, turned the Sky Gods of the Aryans into Brahma, Shiva and Vishnu. The Supreme God Brahma stands outside of creation but also has the role of creator of everything. Vishnu sustains this creation and eventually Shiva will destroy it, returning it to Brahma to begin the cycle again. Male and female, east and west, sky and earth, all joined in one, Hindu, religion.

These Gods had many incarnations, e.g. Krishna is one of the incarnations of Vishnu (c. 850 – 650 B.C.E.) and Hindus believe that these incarnations help mankind evolve to reach mystical Enlightenment, (to return to Brahma, to a release from duality). The religion has a belief in reincarnation, that you are reborn according to your good or bad deeds until karmic balance is achieved. In Hinduism the cow is also considered sacred and not to be eaten (nor are other animals which may even be reincarnations of your ancestors).

The religion also has a rigid caste system where people were born to be priests (Brahmins), warriors, merchants and untouchables. There is also a sense of historical progress, of creation of the universe, its maintenance and its destruction. The priests were able to connect with the Divine Enlightenment and explain it to the rest of society. And those who are not priests can also become Holy Men, Saddhus who meditate in complex Yoga postures, balancing on their hands and heads, invocating deities like Shiva and chanting their mantras. People queue, waiting to be cured of illness, whilst the ash covered gurus pierce their semi-naked bodies, faces and tongues with skewers. They try to raise the "Kundalini", to channel the serpent of spiritual energy up through their bodies, to the head where it can help them attain Enlightenment.

In Hindu temples there are elaborate carvings of the gods. The eyes of these were ritually painted on, to awaken them with life. To some these were living beings but to others they were just a way to gaze upon "Atman," the eternal soul and the complex, intricate carvings represented the infinity, the fullness, of the universal soul that is in everything.

To encompass duality there are two aspects of the deities, e.g. in their benevolent form the sky blue skinned Lord Shiva and his consort Parvati, wear silk robes, and are adorned with silk garlands. They stand together, the perfect celestial couple, eternally in the raptures of their wedding day.

However, Shiva also had another aspect. He will appear, at the end of time, in his most terrifying form, as the Lord of the Dance of destruction. With writhing snakes in his hair and his four arms twisting he will dance within a flaming cosmic wheel. Parvati will also be transformed, into the horrific, four-armed Goddess Kali. With sharp white teeth and dark blue skin, wielding the sword of death and wearing the severed heads of her victims as a necklace. All creation will be consumed by fire in the eternal dance of Shiva. Then all will return to Brahma, the God of Time itself, who existed before good and evil was created. And after this the universe will be created again, in an eternal cycle.

ANCIENT EGYPTIAN AND MESOPOTAMIAN RELIGION

At a similar period to this was the Ancient Egyptian religion (3000 B.C.E. – 300 C.E.). This had many forms but it was always Polytheistic with an extensive Pantheon (range of Gods). It is distinct from Hinduism as there is slightly less focus on mysticism and more on society and the King, worshipped as the Divine Pharaoh. This living Pharaoh was seen as being Horus (the son of the Sun God Ra and the Goddess Isis). When the Pharaoh died he would become Osiris (the Judge of men's souls and would create/father the new Horus with Isis). This life and death cycle also related to the sacrifice of the Apis Bull in the annual fertility cycle that included the flooding of the Nile (necessary for farming).

Parallel to this is the Ancient Near East, Mesopotamia, made up of Assyria, Babylon and Persia. Each nation had its own high bull God of the sun, Assur for the Assyrians, Marduk for the Babylonians and Ahura Mazda for the Persians. And each God had 7 aspects, 7 lesser divinities that they ruled over. Marduk had serpent spirits, Ahura Mazda had winged men and Assur had both.

An example of the region's art are the alabaster friezes from an Assyrian palace at Nimrud. Many of these have protective spirits sent to teach mankind wisdom. They sprinkle water from pine cones onto a date trees. The detailed artistry of these half-life sized men is clear. Their wings show each feather and their hair and goatee beards are formed of tight rings. The thick metre high carvings would have been mounted with hundreds of others besides the steps of the towers, ziggurats. All the figures would face in the direction of the King so that as his subjects walked, they would know who ruled over them. And these Kings were also the state high priests. They were King-Priests, like the Egyptian Pharaoh, and they performed all the major sacrifices, including the annual fertility sacrifice of the Bull God.

ZOROASTRIANISM

The most influential Mesopotamian religion is Zoroastrianism, a religion that began in Ancient Persia with the prophet Zoroaster (c.700 – 600 B.C.E.) Some claim that it is the first monotheism. Zoroaster united the 7 lesser gods by making them aspects, or 7 angels (Yazata), of the One god, Ahura Mazda. This was the God of Good (and light) who was in battle with a lesser God of evil (and darkness) called Spenta Mainyu (also known as Ahriman). Ahura Mazda eventually wins the battle by setting a cosmic trap for Ahriman.

The Zoroastrian faith made sense of famine, drought, floods, storms, earthquakes, pain, lust and hate because Ahura Mazda did not create them, they were made by Ahriman, the Devil, against whom Ahura Mazda battled. This made sense, but it was not strictly Monotheism. It was two Gods, not one, it was Dualism.

A more mystical branch also developed and this was called Zurvanism (after Zurvan the God of Time and father of Ahura Mazda and Spenta Mainyu). Priests of this religion worshipped fire and were called the Magi.

The Persian religion's influence was wide. The Babylonian King, Nebuchadnezzar, captured Jerusalem in 586 B.C.E. and marched the Jewish people in chains to Babylon. Then the Persian King Cyrus the Great (a Zoroastrian) conquered Babylon in the 5th century B.C.E. Cyrus allowed the Jews to rebuild their Temple back in Jerusalem, under the influence of Zoroaster's monotheism.

The influence can be seen visually. The Zoroastrians were the least visual of the Mesopotamians so there aren't any artefacts and they had no images of their God in the Temple, like Judaism (although this prohibition was loose). Despite this the cultures around the Middle East still shared many visual images, e.g. two large, Assyrian Guardian Angels (human headed winged bulls), from the palace of Nimrud, date from around 865 to 850 B.C.E. that guarded doorways to scare away evil spirits. Although these are Assyrian the Jewish scriptures named similar figures Cherubim and placed them as guards of the Tree of Life in the Garden of Eden. They also described these as decoration on the Ark of the Covenant, in which the Jewish Commandments were kept.

In the 4th century B.C.E. Zoroastrianism was spread through the Ancient World by the Macedonian Alexander the Great. He joined the Western (Greek) religions with the Eastern (Persian) religions (including the mysticism of Zurvanism). He believed that he was the incarnation of Mithras, the greatest of the 7 aspects of Ahura Mazda. Mithras was the aspect of fire that came to earth and Mithraism later became the warrior religion of the Roman Empire. It was such a popular religion that every town, city, military garrison and outpost from Syria to Scotland, had a Mithraeum and priest until around 300 C.E.

Little is known about what they believed because most of the evidence was destroyed by Christian zealots. But, basically, Mithras slayed the bull God in a cave and created the world from its body. His followers would sacrifice a bull and share its body and blood in a ritual meal. Alexander was a great warrior and each morning, like Mithras, would sacrifice a bull to the sun. In the British Museum is a Roman statue of a robed soldier slaying a bull. It is a depiction of Mithras, defeating the cosmic bull. He stands over the beast, pulling its head back and piercing its neck with a sword, releasing its vital essences. The bull strains and stretches at its ropes, ready to explode and bellow as a snake drinks the blood pouring from the open wound.

Today Mithraism is a dead religion and Zoroastrianism has only a small number of followers. But it had a final major influence on the 20th century through German philosophy and archaeology.

In his book from the 1880s, "Also Spoke Zarathustra" (another name for Zoroaster) the German philosopher Friedrich Nietzsche argued that the religion of the Jews and Christians was too stifling of evolution. He wanted to replace it with human strength, creativity and will power, the qualities of the new Ubermensch, the Superman. Because Zoroaster was the first prophet of Monotheism, Nietzsche used him to replace Monotheism with his new system of a belief in the Ubermensch.

In the 1870's the archaeologist Heinrich Schliemann discovered the swastika symbol in the site of ancient Troy. Another of the few pieces of archaeological evidence of the swastika in Mesopotamian art is a plate from Samarra (Iraq) c. 5000 B.C.E. that has the Swastika as the sun, surrounded by birds and lower down by fish.

The Nazis later linked it with the swastikas found on ancient German and Mesopotamian pots and created the mythical unity between Germanic, Greek and Indo-Iranian cultures. They believed that an "Aryan" master race originated in northern Europe, and migrated down, through Mesopotamia, into India and Tibet, bringing the Swastika of their Sky God, throughout this region.

The Nazis viewed Hitler as the Fuhrer (Father) a semi-divine incarnation, like one of these Ubermensch, like Alexander the Great. They mixed up a cocktail of lies that ended in the Holocaust, the genocide of the Jews and all non-Aryan people.

JEWISH MONOTHEISM

The Jewish belief that there was just one God, supreme and without equal is believed to have begun with Moses (c.1200 B.C.E.) but archaeological evidence shows the original religion to be polytheistic until after the Jewish people were taken in captivity to Babylon 586 B.C.E. It is then that Judaism took on features of Zoroastrianism. However, it developed into a more radical form of Monotheism.

The Jewish slaves in Babylon knew the importance of freedom. So their God was free and gave freedom to the lowest slave. This God was free to be good but was also free to make mistakes and be a terrible God. This God had created angels and mankind to be free as well. This supports the view that the morality of the Old Testament is questionable, e.g. in II Kings a group of children called the prophet Elisha "bald head" so he cursed them in the name of the Lord and two bears killed them. In Numbers 31 Moses was guilty of ordering infanticide and rape "kill every male among the little ones, and kill every woman that hath known a man by lying with him, but all the women – children, that have not known a man by lying with him, keep alive for yourselves." In Deuteronomy 22 the faithful are told to stone people to death for working on the Sabbath, for not obeying their father and mother and even just for stubbornness.

Artistically there were strict rules against depicting figures in Jewish art, although, there have been many not so strict periods. However, the greatest work of Jewish art was the Temple. The first Temple was built around 1000 B.C.E. by King Solomon and destroyed by the Babylonians in 586 B.C.E. The second was allowed to be rebuilt by the Persian king Cyrus the Great around 516 B.C.E. and was renovated by Herod in 19 B.C.E. but this was then destroyed by the Romans in 70 C.E.

In Solomon's Temple there were lions, bulls and cherubim. Inside the Temple was the Holy of Holies, where the Ark of the Covenant was kept. The Ark of the Covenant was a large, ornate box. On top of it were two Assyrian style Cherubim, which faced each other in prayer, their arched wing-tips touching: 'Make two Cherubim of beaten gold for the two ends of the propitiatory, fastening them so that one Cherub springs direct from each end. The cherubim shall have their wings spread out above, covering the propitiatory with them, they shall be turned toward each other, but with their faces looking toward the propitiatory.' Exodus 25, verses 18-22.

After the destruction of the Second Temple, in the Talmudic period, some synagogues were even ornamented with mosaic figures from the signs of the zodiac, and with the pagan Sun God, Sol Invictus, Apollo, in a chariot drawn by four horses, e.g. from a 5th century synagogue at Sepphoris, Lower Galilee.

Nowadays the Hasidic Jews, the ultra-orthodox, are the strictest against figures, but they still put up posters of their leaders, like Rabbi Solomon Cohen, around Jerusalem.

BUDDHIST MYSTICISM

Whilst the moral and prophetic religion of Judaism developed, Buddhism, a mystical religion, developed, to an extent, from a rejection of the Hindu caste system as it stated that Enlightenment could be achieved by any person if they became dedicated to a meditative life.

Buddha (Siddhartha Gautama) lived in 560 – 480 B.C.E. He renounced his life as a prince and for many years he tried different philosophies and teachings in his quest for Enlightenment, Nirvana. He found this when he created his own system, whilst sitting under a Bo tree. It was then that he ceased to be a slave to his desires and freed himself from the need to be reincarnated. He realised that all of reality has no permanent essence. That even the idea of "self" is an illusion, that the only thing that lasts forever is Nirvana, and we experience its "Oneness" when we realise that all is beyond concepts and opposites (duality).

The psychoanalyst Carl Jung believed in this shared mystical truth behind all religions, and Buddha experienced this truth. He freed his mind from attachment to desire and dwelled in the perfect moment, in pure consciousness in unity with "God." Freud, by contrast, did not believe in this united consciousness. He held that humans were driven by a creative sex drive, Eros, and a death drive, Thanatos. He thought that mystical Nirvana just came from the death drive. But he didn't understand that Nirvana is beyond the opposites (like life and death) imposed by our limited, rational minds.

This split is between Jungian Transcendence (going beyond dual conception to non-dual experience) and Freudian Sublimation (moving from one duality to a higher duality, e.g. from the sexual to the spiritual).

The original Theravada school of Buddhism was a strict practice. It was too strict for most people, who needed help in developing their karma. So a new system was created. The Mahayana (Greater Vehicle), schools of Buddhism are dedicated to the Bodhisattvas. These are Buddhas who gain Enlightenment but choose not to enter complete Nirvana – where they are extinguished from the karmic need to reincarnate. Instead, they become god-like saints who stay to help other beings attain Enlightenment. And in Hinduism the Buddha is seen as an incarnation/ avatar of Vishnu.

This form of Buddhism is more akin to Hinduism in its mix of deities. Artistically this can also be seen. Theravada Buddhism had no images but Mahayana (like Hinduism) has many. In Buddhist statues and Thangka paintings serenity fills the Buddha's face. The plump roundness of his skin echoed in his limbs and body, its smoothness expresses harmonious oneness. The Buddhist doctrine, that there is no soul and that all is emptiness (expressed in the elegant simplicity of smooth golden Buddhas) differs from the infinite complexity of the Hindu Gods (expressed in the intricate detail and variety of forms in Hindu statuary). However, this is just two sides of the same coin, "Nothingness" and "Infinity". These are opposite ways of naming the same experience that is beyond duality.

Buddhism has taken on many cultural influences, e.g. Tibetan Buddhism includes Animistic elements where Tibetan monks, in red headdresses and red robes, chant and play drums, bells and horns for dancers who wear golden masks and whose long wigs trail as they whirl and wail, whilst the prayer wheels keep turning. Another example is Japanese Zen Buddhism, which has strong links to nature (as does Shinto the indigenous Japanese animistic religion) and this is expressed in the minimalism and simplicity of Zen Gardens. This form of Buddhism was influential in America and Europe in the 1950s, 60s and 70s.

CONFUCIANISM & TAOISM

Parallel to the growth of Buddhism was the growth of a new philosophy in China. Animism and ancestor worship were common in China but reform came along with Confucius (c. 551 – 479 B.C.E.) who gave respect to all citizens in a largely secular moral and political system but still respected the belief in Polytheism.

The religious development came with Taoism, which began with Lao-Tzu (pre 2nd century B.C.E.). It is a nature religion that promotes the harmonious balance of opposites, yin and yang (male and female, light and dark). It is one of 3 main religions of China (also Confucianism and Buddhism) that later merged.

This non-dualistic perspective can be seen in the ancient Chinese art of Feng Shui,. The two powerful elements, "Feng" the wind and "Shui" the water, shape mountains, valleys and rivers. When man is in harmony with these then everything, in heaven and on earth, flows in unity.

The most powerful energy (Chi) comes from the breath of the Dragon. It brings good fortune and good luck. Chinese dragons and Chi energy are like the Hindu sacred serpents, the Nagas and the Kundalini power of the snake that rises up through the body towards Enlightenment.

ANCIENT GREEK POLYTHEISM

As mystical religions developed in the East and monotheism developed in the Middle East, rationalism and philosophy developed in the Mediterranean West. This evolved in tandem with the polytheism of the Ancient Greeks. They believed that Zeus, the chief sky God, had defeated the older Gods, led by their father Cronus, the God of Time.

The Greeks were also influenced by the Egyptian and Minoan bull worship religions. In Greek myth the Minoans worshipped a Bull

God of nature and had placed a Minotaur, half-bull and half-man, within a labyrinth. The Minotaur devoured human sacrifices and was eventually killed by Theseus, the future king of the Greek city of Athens. This symbolised the way that the Olympian Gods of Greece, conquered the older, Minoan Gods of Crete. It symbolised how the philosophers of Athens led a new dawn of human reason and a mastery of animal nature.

However, Greek religion had two strands, as described by the 19th century Philosopher Friedrich Nietzsche, who in "The Birth of Tragedy" contrasted Apollo, the Greek God of civilization and law with Dionysus, the God of nature, music, intoxication and mystical ecstasy. Apollo is associated with form and structure and the pure artistic expression of the Apollonian principle is sculpture. By contrast, Dionysis is associated with energy, sexuality, fertility and nature and the pure Dionysian art is music. Nietzsche said that although rational society was Apollonian and that Dionysus was seen as evil nonetheless the true philosopher must embrace Dionysus.

In Greek society this need for a wild, Dionysian element led to the rise of the Mystery Religions that retained elements of Minoan Bull worship. Alexander the Great later united the early Greek mystery religions with Persian and Indian thought in the religion of Mithraism. This was part of a strategy to control the empire that he had conquered and Mithraism flourished until it was replaced with Christianity by Constantine the Emperor of Rome, in the 4th century C.E. Like other Greek and Roman Mystery Religions the priests of Mithraism believed that they could rise to the heavens, through blood sacrifice to help them purify their souls.

Mithras would have been worshipped in a Mithraeum, a Temple to Mithras. These Temples contained a small cave with a sanctuary and altar. Its ceiling decorated with a planetarium of constellations and in the rites of Mithras the followers would eat the body of a sacrificed bull and would drink its blood as they ascended through degrees of initiation, to Gnosis, the highest knowledge.

But the largest influence on Modern Art came from the mystical group of sects named the Gnostics (who originated around the 1st century B.C.E.). One of the cosmologies for Gnosticism was that Sophia, the Goddess of Wisdom, gave birth to the sun, who was a monstrous child and, being ashamed, Sophia wrapped him in the black fabric of the sky. This cosmic abortion was the Demi-urge who began his own evil creation, entrapping divine souls in his earth and proclaimed himself as Lord, over them. And because the Gnostics were persecuted by the early Christian church they associated the Demi-urge with the Hebrew/Christian God Jehovah.

As Greek influence in the Mediterranean grew the Egyptian King Ptolemy I (305-283BCE) changed his God Osiris to Serapis (related to the Apis sacred bull) to unite the Egyptian and Greek subjects. Osiris was linked with their oldest sun god Zeus Helios, and (to mystically unite opposites) also with Pluto, ruler of the underworld. Statues showed him in Grecian style with long feminine hair and a heavy beard whose androgynous form was hidden under flowing robes and his body is encircled by the coils of a great serpent. Serapis became identified with the time God Aion, another father God of Time, like Zurvan of the Zoroastrians.

CHRISTIANITY

Christianity was began as a small Jewish sect by the Jewish prophet Jesus Christ (4 B.C.E. – 29 C.E.). The religion later became concerned with Pagan ideas of a man-god who was sacrificed and resurrected to save the souls of believers. And the theology in the New Testament clearly states that Christ is God. But this was influenced by ideas that came from Saint Paul who had originally persecuted Christians for the Romans and was influenced by many Graeco–Roman ideas.

However, many early Christians would have believed in strict Monotheism, in the divine "unity" of God, just like the Jews. As a Jew Jesus he would have been brought up to believe in One God and so many of the early Christian Jews would have been Unitarians, seeing Christ as a man, a prophet, not a divinity. However, when the Bible scriptures were set in the 4th century, at the Council of Nicea by theologians in the Holy Roman Empire, the Pagan influence won out. Ancient Roman Polytheism was influenced by Greek religion and the Greek gods and was also influenced by Mithraism – from

Bull Gods and Zoroastrians. The pagan blood rites won out over the Jewish influences and Christianity became another version of the old religions of Dionysus, Mithras and Horus.

Christian ideas of an incarnate God, his virgin birth and sacrificial death all derive from Polytheism. The Greek God of wine, Dionysus, was fathered by a God and died a violent death then came to life again. The same with the Roman God Mithras, who died a violent death for man's sins and descended to the underworld, then rose again into Heaven. The Christian concept of Heaven is derived from the Greek Elysium Fields (Jews just have earthly resurrection) and the Christian holy day is Sunday, the day of the Roman sun God, Sol Invictus, instead of Saturday, the Jewish Sabbath. Christ's birthday, the 25th of December, is also the same as the Roman Sun God and the Egyptian god, Horus.

The early Egyptian church also made Christ resemble their own ancient deities. Christ, the God King, born after God miraculously impregnated the Virgin Mary, was like Horus, the God King, born after the God Osiris miraculously impregnated the Goddess Isis. When Horus died he became Osiris, (like Christ became one with God) before rising again as the new Pharaoh. The Virgin Mary was also venerated, just like the Isis, and this only ended when Emperor Constantine made Christianity the state religion of the Holy Roman Empire in 312 C.E.

The Romans finally accepted Christianity because it had swept across Europe and Asia so Constantine had to accept Christianity to keep his Empire from falling apart. But he transformed it into a stately Roman warrior religion, like that of the sun Gods Sol Invictus and Mithras. Instead of spreading Christ's message of "love your enemy" Constantine's Holy warriors would kill their enemies then pray for them afterwards.

The influence is clear in churches across the   West Bank / Israel / Palestine where there are many churches dedicated to Saint George. In these are images of Saint George, on a white horse, killing a dragon with his spear. Saint George of Lydda, was a 3rd century Roman Christian soldier and martyr. George and Constantine, the future Emperor of Rome, were both soldiers and friends. When

George became a Christian he was tortured and executed because he would not follow the Emperor Diocletian's orders to persecute Christians. So when Constantine became Emperor in 306, he made the martyred George a Saint and the "Champion Knight of Christendom." He became an icon for the new warrior Christianity that replaced Mithraism (the old religion of the Roman soldiers). Saint George became the example for Holy Christian warriors to follow, including the mediaeval Knights Templar who bore his red cross upon their vestments.

Saint George, the Roman soldier who followed Mithras before converting to Christianity, was the perfect Christian soldier, a role model to gain Roman converts, and his slaying the Dragon, the Serpent, replaced the image of Mithras killing the primeval bull. And when Constantine's mother, Queen Helena, rebuilt the churches destroyed by Diocletian and destroyed almost all traces of Mithraism. She dedicated many of the churches to St. George. And to keep the Empire unified the worship of Mithras was replaced, banned. Then, at the Council of Nicea, 325 C.E., a single Christian doctrine, the Nicene Creed was produced. This made the Holy Trinity, the unity of God the Father, the Son and the Holy Spirit, an essential part of Christian doctrine.

The Unitarians, who believed that Jesus Christ was just a man, and the mystics, who believed that Jesus Christ was completely divine, were excommunicated, beaten, intimidated, kidnapped, imprisoned and killed.

The pagan faith that Constantine adapted later split into Orthodox and Catholic with the death of Emperor Theodosius the Great in 395. That is when the Holy Roman Empire was divided into Western and Eastern halves, each under its own Emperor, each with different rites and doctrines.

This split reached its high point in the Great Schism of 1054, when the Western, Catholic Church changed the doctrine of the Nicene Creed to say that the Holy Spirit proceeds "from the Father and the Son," not just "from the Father." This minor change created a split so great that in 1204 the Catholic Crusaders attacked Constantinople, the capitol of their Orthodox brethren.

Artistically, the early Christians had very few images, and these were mainly in tombs, because they followed Jewish prohibitions or because the early church was persecuted. Then the Holy Roman Christianity began to use art, derived from pagan Rome, revoking Jewish prohibitions against images of God because God now had a human form, Jesus Christ, so He could now be represented, like a Roman God. The problem though, was that no original images of Christ existed. This was overcome when the first Byzantine Icon was created in the 4th century, taken from a reputedly miraculous image imprinted onto a shroud of cloth that had been pressed onto Christ's wet face after his crucifixion. The Orthodox tradition kept the use of these Icons, flat images, whilst the Catholics began to create ever more elaborate statues and paintings.

Then, with the invention of the printing press, the Bible was widely translated and distributed around Europe. As a result people, like Martin Luther, began to make their own Protestant Christian interpretations of the scriptures. They rejected the elaborate Catholic rituals in the Reformation, destroying icons in churches. However, there was still a tradition of narrative imagery in Protestantism.

Herbert L. Kessler argues that Icons presented the danger that they would be seen as personifications of the person portrayed in them and become icons to be adored, but narrative art made this worship less likely. So even in periods of iconoclasm the largely illiterate culture needed narrative images for showing doctrine and belief (2). Only more extreme, moralistic Protestants, like the Puritans, rejected all imagery.

And as more books were printed people grew further away from the traditional belief in God and this was the beginning of Modernism, with its science, rationality and abstract spirituality.

ISLAM

Islam begins with Muhammed (570 – 632 C.E.). The Qur'an is believed to be a revelation of a moral and religious code of conduct from God, to Muhammed, through the Angel Gabriel, and it is believed that there is no poetry more beautiful. As the Qur'an says:

"And if you are in doubt about what We have revealed to Our worshiper (Muhammed Peace Be Upon Him), then produce a chapter like it."

Mecca was the site of the Kaaba, believed to be where Abraham (the ancestor of both Muslims and Jews) built a shrine to Allah. It was where Polytheists had set up idols of Baal, the Bull God of the sun. Muhammed preached there for ten years but was persecuted for telling the truth, so he left for Medinah, in 622 C.E., then returned to conquer Mecca with an army of believers, in 630 C.E., smashing the idols as false gods.

Muslim art is associated with architecture and calligraphy, e.g. the Haram esh Sharif, the Most Noble Sanctuary in Jerusalem, where dazzling light reflects on the golden Dome of the Rock, an architectural shrine, that stands on the Sanctuary. Around it is a garden paradise, where avenues of tall trees and marble fountains stand on a plateaux of limestone paving and stepped terraces. The nearby Al Aqsa mosque is free of images, statues and furniture. Here nothing detracts from the worship of Allah. Classically Islamic, decorative splendour (marble walls, columns and arches, golden mosaics, the floral designs and the swirling Corinthian capitals) join with an economy of design would suit a modern architect.

But the Arabic inscriptions, of the names of God and verses from the Qur'an, are the real artworks. These are the Holy words and poetry put into a visual form. The high stemmed letters, curved with small, tight, round consonants, to form shapes of divine beauty. This is the only way that "Allah", the most infinite being, whose greatness is beyond any depiction, could be shown as the tradition holds that it is idolatrous to use icons and human forms to depict God.

This is also the site of the old Jewish Temple, of which the Western Wall is the main area that remains. Muslims built the Dome of the Rock here because in 621 C.E. Muhammed made his Night Journey, on a winged creature, with the angel Gabriel. On his night journey he spoke with Allah and led prayers with Adam, Idris the prophet of Noah, Abraham, Aaron the High Priest of Moses and Moses. He showed that he is the last true Prophet, the "Seal of the Prophets."

The split between Sunni and Shia started when Muhammed died. The Shia said that Muhammed's son-in-law should lead the Muslims and the Sunnis said that Muhammed's follower Abu Bakr, should be the leader. The division grew when the Shia said that their first twelve leaders, Imams were divinely infallible whilst the Sunnis said that only Muhammed was infallible. Now they pray in different ways. The Shia believe that the 12th Imam will return as a leader called the Mahdi.

Sunni Muslims also have a ban on idolatry. However, pictures of the Prophet, surrounded with flames, on the winged beast of the Night Journey come from the eastern Shia Muslims, who were influenced by the Persian, fire worshipping, Zoroastrians. A mystical branch of Islam also developed out of the Shia sect and this was called Sufism. It had a focus on poetry, beauty and monastic devotions.

FREEMASONRY

In 1119 C.E. the European Crusaders slaughtered everyone in Jerusalem, whether Muslim, Jew or Christian. Then they established camp there, supported with money from wealthy European bankers until 1187 C.E. The Crusaders were supported by Venetian bankers who covered Italy and northern Europe with their modern banking system, lending money with interest. It was usury, forbidden by the church, but this was sidestepped with clever loopholes.

In the Holy Land" the European Stonemasons learned about Islamic architecture. They became technicians who saw God as the Master Builder. They were commissioned to construct the Catholic Cathedrals of Europe and they grew rich and powerful. They helped to begin the expansion of western learning that led to the Renaissance and their knowledge was not just technical, it was also spiritual and mystical.

Then, in 1305, the Kings of France and England rounded up the Templars, confiscated their wealth and charged them with Satanism. The Kings claimed that the Templars had found the secret teachings of King Solomon's master mason, Hiram Abif, a pagan from Tyre, under the Temple in Jerusalem, and has begun to worship the Pagan horned Devil God.

The Masons continued to practice until the 16th century, when Henry VIII broke from the Catholic Church in Rome. Then many of the Masonic Lodges were destroyed, and their finances seized. It was after this that Freemasonry began. Instead of being a trade organisation for stone masons Freemasonry was an organisation open to merchants, entrepreneurs and businessmen who were independent of the state and were interested in the ancient spiritual truths the Masons had uncovered. The symbols of Masonry, like the square, compasses, level, plumb-line and the chisel were used in secret ceremonies and rituals.

The first step was to become an Apprentice. Later you can become a Master Mason, and progress to earn titles like Temple workman, Israel tribesman, High Priest of the Jews, King Hiram of Tyre and Knight Templar. The titles were dramatised in rituals of the climbing of degrees of learning of the secret knowledge, the Gnosis of the Masons.

QABBALAH (JEWISH MYSTICISM)

The Masons claimed to have secret teachings passed down from Moses to the Jewish people. These teachings are the Qabbalah and they have influenced Judaism to such an extent that they are now mainstream teachings within Judaism. The Qabbalah is the secret teachings encoded in the 22 letters of the Jewish alphabet as each letter had its own number used in the coding of the Torah. Scholars hold that the Jewish thinker Maimonides introduced the Qabbalah to Europe in the Middle Ages. But it is believed that the Qabbalah also came out of the Jewish people's time in Persia and Egypt. Its 22 letters are "paths" between 10 "emanations," aspects of God, up the Tree of Life. This journey begins in the material emanation, Malkuth, but the goal is the top emanation, Kether.

Maimonides believed that God created man with angelic consciousness. But mankind fell when his female side was tempted by the serpent, bringing knowledge of good and evil. Forgiveness and righteousness now come when we return to the original Oneness of God, to the absolute reality, where all opposites are united in balance. This is a mystical way of thinking, with a God who is beyond good and evil. It's Pantheism and not Monotheism. And the

Persian split between Zoroastrianism and Zurvanism (its mystical branch) is mirrored in Prophetic Judaism and in Qabbalism a mystical strand which developed in the Middle Ages.

WORLD RELIGION CONCLUSION

The human connection to Divinity has been attempted through a religious relation to external Gods or through a mystical connection to the whole universe. Initially these 2 areas co-existed in Animism but as civilization developed the conceptual difference between the 2 perspectives became articulated and expressed in different cultures.

For the Hindus and Egyptians the external Gods became ways of expressing the mystical for ordinary believers. Meanwhile the Gods became the objects of absolute moral veneration for the Zoroastrians and Jews, whilst a mystical doctrine became a secret teaching for their Priests. Buddhists tried to make the mystical perspective into a coherent, rational system but the focus on external Gods returned in Mahayana Buddhism. The Greeks and Romans had a focus on rational enquiry and also had a balance between the worship of the Gods and the mystical mystery religions. When Jewish based Christianity adapted Roman ideas these mystery religions were forced into the background, though they were still present in a ritual form (taken from Mithraic rites). Islam moved further away from any Polytheism in a strict focus on God and a rejection of idols. Islam balanced with a mystical branch in Sufism. This interest in mysticism also resurfaced in Christianity and Judaism through contact with Islamic culture (who had preserved Greek and Roman writings) and gave rise to Freemasonry and Qabbalah.

With this overview we can now look at how Religion and Mysticism have influenced Modern Art.

MODERN ART

38

DEFINITIONS OF ART

"Art" is a notoriously difficult term to define and to define art as primarily aesthetic objects that are non-useful is a modern definition that is a result of art-objects ceasing to have a pre-modern relevance and function. Thus I would like to define art also by the processes by which the object is created. Thus I define "art" as being any form of creative activity that involves a degree of skill or ingenuity, where marvel at the beauty within this created object is a major purpose. Therefore this includes objects used in ritual or industrial design, which can be admired as works of beauty. However, art is not just about objects, it is also about the processes that have no end object and this can include the ritual and industrial processes themselves.

Definitions of "art" also depend on what the use of the art work is. As such, religious and modern art are very different. We will fist construct a definition of religious art which will then enable us to analyse modern art by looking at the beliefs that it rejects and also the beliefs that it holds.

A definition of art should include a list of forms, e.g. painting, sculpture, ceramics, installations, music, dance, ritual, performance, drama, environment, architecture, literature and fashion,

DEFINITIONS OF RELIGIOUS ART

Painting, in a modern context, is usually to a flat canvas or wall although sculpture, architecture and many objects can also be painted. The painting can be abstract designs or representational of objects, figures and stories.

Because of their life-like qualities sculptures were used to represent Gods and so Idols became the point of contact for mankind to God. There may have been abstract stylisation of the Gods although it is rare to find complete abstraction as purely geometric objects were usually functional, e.g. jewellery and ceramics.

Installations in Modern Art are created environments, often abstract with colours and designs. It is not just a theatrical stage where a drama is displayed. The whole body of the participant is involved and the subject-object distinction is broken down as the viewer becomes part of the work that they experience. The music and primal colours/shapes involved also relate to basic instincts so as to by-pass the conscious mind.

Performance can be in front of an audience or involve the audience. When dance is involved the participant moves around and experiences space in a primal way.

The way that these polarities of installation, performance and sculpture were linked was through ritual. The temple housed artworks and inside this space the believer interacted with the statues and icons through religious ritual drama and role play.

Sacred literature and ritual words were involved. These narrative tools combine with the music and by putting on sacred vestments and jewellery the Priest and believers enter completely into the drama – whilst using designed ritual objects like cups and knifes.

The ultimate form of ritual is sacrifice, when a life is taken using a sacred knife, on a sacred altar, in a sacred space. Communion of the blood of this sacrifice then involves the believer in the transformational energy and power of the ritual.

In religious cultures art and religion were interconnected. Religion was weaved into every aspect of life and art was an integral part of this. Many secular political figures were sanctified in their office and treated as religious figures (e.g. the King or Pharaoh). Rituals pervaded society so even ordinary domestic items for eating were sanctified. Art and religion only became more separate as modern art developed.

So we see that religious art is a combination of art-forms and ideas that evolve through tradition. Performance and architecture are integral to religious art and the gallery has replaced the temple and interactive art performances have replaced rituals.

An artist might even be seen as a Priest, but this is only really the case in performance art if the artist is deliberately playing this role in their own created religion or if the artist's own body is a self-administered sacrifice (in the self-mutilation of modern performance art).

Rather, the Modern artists can have two kinds of religious roles. The first is like the Prophets of a religion, presenting ideas and visions, when they do work that has a critical message (like the Iconoclastic Jewish prophets). The second is like a Saint or like a God who is venerated. And they become like Saints when their artworks is treated like relics of the Saints in a church or if they are treated as God like celebrities. Then their artworks are also treated like manifestations of their Divinity. Artists can be in touch and at one with divine inspiration and this makes curators treat them and their work as semi-Divine. The priest also sanctified the art/Icon that is made by the artist, and turned it into a manifestation of God. So, in a modern context, curators of artists' work are like Priests who give the artists and their work a Divine status.

Thus the artist can be like a Prophet or a Saint/Demi-God. If art work has a religious approach and content it does not mean that it belongs to a religious venue and not an art gallery. I argue that art that just illustrates religion can still be art, through the skilful processes used in its creation. The religious content needs to challenge the very nature of art and/or the artistic content needs to challenge the very nature of religion. As such the artist can be like the Prophet who challenges theological structures and the Saint/Demi-God who performs creative miracles within those structures.

However, there is a tension between the two as the prophet challenges art that claims to be as important as God and challenges any artist who sees themselves as semi-Divine.

Nonetheless, the relationship between art and divine status is close. God is often seen as the creator of the Universe and many of God's prophets may have been artists. The Jewish prophet Moses may have been an architect (and a Master Mason who carved the 10 commandments into stone), the Christian prophet Jesus Christ may have been a carpenter (in his father's trade) and Krishna (the Hindu incarnation of Vishnu) played the flute.

However, the real art of the prophets lay in words. The New Testament, the Torah, the Qur'an, the Guru Grant Sahib, the Bhagavad Gita. All were the words and laws of God. Therefore the religious artwork, closest to the "logos," to the "word" of God is poetry. As such it is Mohammed who was a poet whose artwork may have a form that is closest to the Divine.

However, a religious poetry or scriptures are not a work of "modern" literature, whose vain writers were greedy for fame. Rather, it is a Holy book, where the writer is the voice-piece for the Divine, where religion is more important than art or the artist.

Kings have lost most of their Divine status, however, as artists now have a semi-religious status whoever commissions their work (the patron) is key to religious, modern and contemporary art. And this is tied up with political developments. The Emperor/King would commission religious art in the pre-modern religious society. State politicians and private financiers would commission non-religious art in modern society. This continued in postmodern society but now we see a rising mixture of both religious and non-religious art in a postmodern society. In this global economy the private financiers, rulers and leaders from the developing economies of religious countries (in Brazil, Russia, India and China) jostle to create their own political, social and economic narratives for a world religion.

HISTORY OF RELIGIOUS ART

To understand religious art we need to look at how religions developed through the dynamic relationship between religion and art.

People in tribal societies were united in Animism but schizophrenically fluctuated between the mystical and moral consciousnesses in meditation/chanting and magic. Animism involved worshipping Gods but humans took more control through magic, where they channelled mystical energy into forms through images. Finding the correct words and images became important to unleashing latent powers. When religions focussed more on mystical and moral elements in their religions then corresponding art forms were uncovered.

Both moral religion and mystical spirituality are essential parts of the human psychology and throughout history the psyche has subconsciously used art to balance these extremes. The mystical relates to abstract design (i.e. appreciated as an immediate experience) and the moral relates to figurative, narrative art about Gods with human attributes).

An abstract design that arises immediately from unconscious energy is symbolised as purely aesthetic. Here the person is intimately connected to nature. A figurative representation of nature that is external to the person comes from a self-conscious subject-object relationship. By representing the Gods as an object then a subject-object relationship is created for the viewer. These objects stand separate from nature. They are a form imposed upon matter, and relate to historical beings with moral, dual, meaningful, conceptual structures.

In ritual, primitive creativity linked the more mystical aesthetic process (e.g. meditation, music, dance and design) are linked with the more moral, narrative, meaningful products, (e.g. Icons, figures and statues). Ritual was the original common point between abstract nature and figurative narrative but humanity advanced into both extremes.

Different cultures developed a variety of ways in which they balanced these opposites. And this depended on whether they thought that art A) directly manifested the Divine or B) that the Divine is held as being too sacred to directly manifest so is manifested in an opposite artistic form (although religions can be a combination of both as in Hinduism and, later, Buddhism). Given that the Divine is either 1 (mystical abstract) or 2 (moral figurative) there are 4 possible combinations.

(A1) the mystical is directly expressed in abstract design, music and dance e.g. Hindu mandalas or in the artwork of some Modern artists.

(A2) the moral is directly expressed in figurative narrative painting and sculpture e.g. Greek polytheism.

(B1) the mystical is indirectly expressed in figurative narrative art eg. Hindu and Buddhist statues. Thus abstract, mystical religions balanced with figurative art forms (as in Buddhist and Hindu mysticism).

(B2) the moral is indirectly expressed in abstract art eg. Islamic and Jewish architectural design. These moral religions (a God with human qualities) balance with abstract design and the prohibition against making images (as in Jewish and Islamic monotheism).

Given this mapping of the way that world religion has unconsciously attempted to synthesise the perspectives we can identify a general trend - although there are exceptions where religions can be made up of a variety of views, e.g. the Hindu and Buddhist mandalas are abstract direct manifestations of mystical principles, whereas Hindu and later Buddhist myths are narratives represented in figurative art so as to be popular embodiment of these mystical principles.

Greek and Roman art, religion and culture (A2) also provides a notable exception to being stuck within this dynamic. In its pantheon (range of gods) are the oracles of revelation and the Muses, who inspire the arts, and who are the daughters of the Sky God Zeus (who defeated his father Cronus, the God of Time). Greek culture consciously viewed art and creativity as divine and used art to directly express the Greek Polytheism manifesting its figurative Gods directly in its art forms and eventually tried to balance this figurative spirituality by moving to the abstract principles of science and philosophy that developed into Modernism.

However, before this modern development Christianity dominated Western Culture. Christianity gave a balance of the figurative and abstract aspects of the psyche by joining Graeco-Roman and Jewish thinking. It joined the apparently contradictory images of the Gods (Greek) with a rejection of any such images (Jewish) in the doctrine of the Trinity. The Romans brought their Gods to life by using statues in ritual theatre, in dramatic enactments of the stages of life. And the Roman focus on God incarnated as Jesus Christ was represented in figurative Icons whilst the Jewish view of God was generally a non-incarnate God - the Father and was not to be represented.

So the art of the Jews was too abstract for the Holy Roman Empire. Thus they converted the Jewish God into a Roman God by incarnating the Jewish God into the human Jesus Christ in the doctrine of the Trinity.

This means that, in our model, Christianity is a mix of Greek (A2) and Jewish (B2) perspectives. It is split between the abstract Father and figurative Son in the doctrine of the Trinity. The abstract Jewish God of power was converted to the Roman Pantocrator, ruler of all, and represented in the human form as Jesus Christ. However, this Trinity created its own complex internal dynamic. And the rational Graeco-Roman mind was slowly moving towards direct abstraction.

The Renaissance gave balance in a Humanism by focussing on the importance of human thinking in abstract technology, science and the occult quest for mystical transcendence. A search parallel with the development of Jewish Qabbalism. The Humanists looked at the natural powers of human reason and artistry in philosophy and the teachings of the classics. Artistically thery explored geometric perspective and classical mythology in landscape and cityscape scenes. They were freeing themselves to analyse and explore the possibility of art outside of a religious context. The Graeco-Roman representational styles were re-discovered by artists such as Michaelangelo, Leonardo da Vinci etc and harnessed for neo-classical themes. However, their deep beliefs were still abstract and hierarchical, with a focus on neo-Platonic mysticism.

The more personal and human element of Christianity came with the invention of the printing press - which led to the printing of the Bible in local languages. This gave individuals the opportunity to interpret scriptures without the need for a Priest (who would read them in Latin). The Protestants rejected the Catholic focus on the state God, the controlling Father (who was represented in art), and focussed on the personal Jesus Christ (and refused to allow him to be represented in art). These Protestants, who rejected the political influence of the Catholic Church, had a personal relationship to an incarnate figurative Christ so they psychologically balanced by rejecting icons, in favour of abstract/natural simple design.

As a result this contributed to the rise of the Eighteenth century Scientific revolution and Rational Enlightenment (not to be confused with mystical Enlightenment). Early scientists still retained faith in the figure of Jesus Christ but looked at God's creation in the quest for the abstract truths behind nature. The art of the time focussed on landscape and Romanticism as Northern European society was moving to try and encompass an appreciation of the natural world. And faith in the new, successful scientific Modernism, would gradually undermine and replace many peoples' Christianity with a belief in abstract mysticism.

DEFINITIONS OF MODERNISM

Now we have almost reached a point where we can begin to understand the religious bases of Modern Art.

Before we continue we will look at definitions of modernisation, Modernity and Modernism. Modernisation, usually means to bring things up to date with what is the most efficient and latest object or process, Modernity is another name for the modern age which is the result of modernisation and Modernism is the set of underlying assumptions involved in following modernisation and Modernity.

There are multiple perspectives on what are the underlying assumptions of Modernism but the most obvious relates to science and technology. Modernists sought the principles underlying reality in abstract, analytical, mathematical, geometric and law-like orderings. This philosophy is often associated with Sir Isaac Newton's view of the world as being mechanistic and Modernism often involved a search for universal answers, formal qualities and definitions in a "Grand Narrative" of progress through science industrialisation and rationality. Modernists claimed that science needed no justifying as it progressed towards a complete knowledge, united in common goals and methods and of benefit to humanity.

DEFINITIONS OF MODERN ART

Broadly speaking, the innovation of Modern art was that it has been concerned primarily with questions of form and aesthetics. It made any moral purpose into a secondary concern and was "art for art's sake". In its pure form it had no function, it was just aesthetic. Consequently much industrial and architectural design of the period was minimal, emphasising the pure functionality of the objects.

James Elkins notes that what is classed as "art" is so varied that almost anything can be included within the term. The only way to encompass all of the works is to give a social definition for the term "art" is work that is produced by artists, exhibited in galleries or published in art magazines (3). This apparently postmodern analysis means that there is no objective standard and that what is art is controlled by a small, often biased, group of people and that many popular objects of a religious or artistic nature are excluded.

My own view, as will be explained later is that art can be regulated and classified in much the same manner as any other area of knowledge, just that the social interests, that Elkins mentions, have a vested interest in not allowing these classifications to be made. This is because regulation will reduce the monetary value of works in their collections and will require an overhaul of practices and standards in the art-world to ensure that they are more transparent and equitable.

Cynthia Freeland attempts a non-social definition which explains great variety and a freedom for any message to be contained within a work of art. She identifies two strands of art, those containing expression and those containing content. Expression is the emotive method by which an artwork is created and the content is the intellectual meaning invested in the final product. This content can also include the analysis of the nature of art and art-forms (which differs from a purely aesthetic appreciation of a work as it is an analysis of aesthetics). It was the Greek, and later Islamic, interest in academic learning that set the dynamic for a Renaissance investigation into the principles of art and perspective. This study and innovation within art became part of the content and interest in art.

This definition of art is still very general but with it we have some structure for analysis.

An artist who marks a turning point from Christian and Classical narrative art is William Blake, 1757-1827. His works adapted passages from the Christian Bible into a personal, mystical mythology and expressed these with vital energy.

"The Number of the Beast Is 666", by Blake, takes Revelation 13 verses 11-12 & 18. "The Red Dragon and the Beast from the sea are joined by a Beast who comes up out of the earth. The Beast will have two horns like a lamb and will speak as a dragon. He will cause the earth and all who dwell therein to worship the first Beast and will make fire come down from heaven." "Here is wisdom. Let him that hath understanding count the number of the Beast, for it is the number of a man, and his number is Six hundred three-score and six."

In the painting, bathed in fire, a red dragon-figure with seven horned heads rages angrily above a Beast that rises from the sea. Between them is a creature with a sheep-like skull. Their colours and swirls are dynamic, powerful, and malevolent. It is a small pen and ink watercolour. Its distorted neo-classical figures contrast and blend, almost child-like in style. They are aggressive monstrosities that stare out.

The energy and vitality coupled with the uncompromising vision (from the New Testament) speaks directly and is timeless. And yet Blake was a visionary artist who made his own personal mythology with two main characters Urizen and Los. Urizen (reason) was like the Old Testament God, Jehovah, the Demi-urge, whose Laws and idea of 'sin' were oppressive traps to prevent people enjoying earthly pleasures. Only Los (imagination - a mystical version of a Christ-like figure) could save mankind.

In another small watercolour, "The Ancient of Days" 1824, the hand of the bearded Urizen makes a compass that emanated golden lines. Like Jehovah he sets out the creation of the Universe. This design resembled the cover of Isaac Newton's scientific treatise, "Principia Mathematica". Blake believed that science, like Urizen, trapped men's souls in a prison of rationalism and materialism which only Los, imagination, could overthrow. Los would bring man back into unity with the Divine through his son Orc, a serpent of revolutionary energy. Orc would help Los unite with his female aspects and eventually even unite with Urizen.

Blake's images, are illustrations of the New Testament, but the text gives a message of spiritual unity, of Eastern mysticism over Western religious imagery. Blake's vision marked the start of an era when artists tried to update religious ideas. Artists would reject the scientific world view as being too restrictive (though they still adopted science's freedom of enquiry). This close relationship between science, mysticism and art would grow as modernism developed.

Western society would begin to trust artists, not priests and ministers, as the people with access to spiritual revelation. Artists now had the prophet's right to decree on issues of faith, and eventually following on from Romanticism (as we shall see) under the philosophy of Nietzsche, they would proclaim that God was dead. And art would become all about aesthetic expression (the direct art of mysticism) and narrative content would be dismissed.

ROMANTICISM

In the next era the Romantic artists turned Blake's heavenly scenes into earthly scenes as the Romantics began to paint nature and investigate the nature of painting.

Marc C. Taylor thinks that the Romantic conception of art has dominated modern art theory and that pivotal to understanding the romantic conception of art is the philosophy of Immanuel Kant. Taylor describes Kant's philosophy of aesthetics in Kant's "Critique of Pure Reason" (4). Kant argued that the information that we collect through our various senses (sight, touch, hearing etc), is ordered into understandable experiences by processes of reasoning. We pass from this personal sense data to a rational understanding of the data via the imagination in an act of synthesis. This synthesis is fundamental to our ability to experience the world.

The experience of the sublime is when data is presented to thought exceeds all thought. The mind is unable to conceive of the size or force of an experience and horror at the inadequacy of the understanding is felt in face of the vast and dreadful open possibility of the imagination.

Two early nineteenth century philosophers who tried to fill the space generated by an experience of the sublime, were F.W.J. Schelling and G.W.F. Hegel. Schelling proposed a link between the internal and external in an intellectual intuition that the individual is identical with absolute being, in a pantheistic, mystical identity with the whole universe. So even if something is beyond our understanding it is still ultimately part of absolute being. In contrast Hegel proposed an intellectual joining of subject and object. In a system, based on rational argument (rather than on intuition). This system showed a historical progression to the idea of the individual as identical with absolute being (5). So this Romantic search for uniting humans and nature was either through a direct experience, like Schelling's philosophy, or an intellectual system of thought, like Hegel's philosophy.

It was philosophies like Schelling's that initially influenced artists. A good example of an art work relating to this is Caspar David Friedrich's. Joseph Leo Koerner, Assistant Professor of Fine Art at Harvard University, argues that around 1700 C.E. landscape painting was still concerned with religious morality and allegorical painting (6) but in Friedrich's "Wanderer above the Sea of Fog", c.1818 a figure serves as an indication of our relation to the landscape and the infinite, but at one remove.

The lone figure, dressed in a knee length coat, stands on top of a mountain, looking across a sea of clouds from which peaks arose. The figure has his back to the viewer and was ready to merge into the horizon, into the home of the Gods. The figure is turned like a God and can see the infinite yet also represents our exclusion from it. This figure is paradoxically both part of the landscape and not part of it (7). The viewer approaches a pantheistic dissolution into the infinite background of nature by way of a figure whose back is turned to us (8).

The work is at the crossroads between ideas of the individual, nation, religion and God and a pantheistic union with nature. The contrast is between the solo figure and the whole landscape. This self is then annihilated in the work of the English painter, J.M.W. Turner. Turner integrated with nature, preferring the aesthetic expression over interpretative meaning.

Turner's subjects were shipwrecks, fires, natural catastrophes, and natural phenomena such as sunlight, storm, rain, and fog. And he used these to express the moods of Nature. In his later work he was fascinated by the violent power of the sea, as seen in "Dawn after the Wreck" 1840 and "The Slave Ship" 1840. In removing narrative he tried to create a purely immediate, non-anthropomorphic expression that allowed access to the natural world. In this way Turner indicated the vulnerability of human beings amid the 'sublime' nature of the world.

Turner was also expressing spirituality in the world, rather than representing objects that he saw. He was evoking a pure light by using shimmering colour. This light was to Turner the emanation of God's spirit and in his later paintings he left out objects and focussed on light on water and on the radiance of skies and fires. In "Rain, Steam and Speed - The Great Western Railway" (1844) he used a watercolour technique with oil paints to create ephemeral atmospheric effects where the objects are barely recognizable. These late paintings appear 'impressionistic' and were a forerunner of the French Impressionists, such as Claude Monet.

This change in art practice towards abstraction was also caused by technological invention of photography which removed the need for realism in art. Art began to move away from the copying of reality which could be done with photographic images and became a way of investigating and studying reality. As a result artists became free to be more abstract or more expressive.

EARLY MODERNIST ART

The abstract art of Paul Cezanne came from his study of naturally occurring forms by breaking them down into into their geometric essentials of the cylinder, the sphere, the cone. He worked from direct observation and developed a solid, sculptural and architectural style of painting. "Les Grandes Baigneuses" 1898–1905 explored the way that our binocular vision provides us with spatial relationships, e.g. depth, between objects. This led him to overlap the outlines of forms so as to capture the different viewpoints of both eyes. This transforms earlier ideals of single-point perspective and was to influence the Cubists.

Similarly Vincent van Gogh created abstractions but his work was expressive, rather than analytic, e.g. "Wheatfield with Crows" 1890. This work vibrates in a unified field, in a transformed reality. The wheat-field displays the same brush strokes as the sky and the crows. All is joined in one foreboding reality. Writing in 1890, Van Gogh said that he had become absorbed "in the immense plain against the hills, boundless as the sea, delicate yellow" (9). He wrote of "vast fields of wheat under troubled skies", and that he did not "need to go out of my way to try and express sadness and extreme loneliness".

Van Gogh was a former trainee Priest and missionary. He began to study to become an artist to try and understand what the great artists tell us that leads to God. Van Gogh's search was emotional and expressive.

An alternative strand to the analytic and expressive was the symbolic. In Primitivism the new symbolism, the style of the art also helps to convey ideas. This art was partly a sociological and anthropological study. It was a back to basics quest to find religious and cultural answers in Animism. Paul Gauguin, a Post-Impressionist painter created his Primitivism in the late 19th century. This art movement was characterized by exaggerated body proportions, animal totems, geometric designs and stark contrasts inspired by the raw power and simplicity of the art of foreign cultures. Living in Tahiti, he painted "Where Do We Come From" 1897 and other works full of quasi-religious symbolism and exotic view of the Polynesian native peoples. He used primitive, bold, colours and images, recalling an Eden-like natural simplicity of mankind.

At the same time, this reference to the primitive, original man had also been explored in Western Philosophy by the German philosopher Friedrich Nietzsche, in his book from the 1880s, "Also Spoke Zarathustra", another name for Zoroaster. He used Zoroaster (arguably the first prophet of monotheism) as a literary device to replace God and monotheism with a belief in the "Will to Power," the "survival of the fittest" and the need for hardness, strength and cruelty. He saw Christianity as weak and the religion of the oppressed that came out of the Jewish religion, which came out of slavery in Egypt and Babylon. Instead he wanted a new breed of men, creative geniuses, Ubermensch, Supermen, beyond the petty rules of the herd. For Nietzsche Zarathustra was a dancer who leapt, somersaulted and beckoned with his wings, ready for flight.

Adolph Hitler misinterpreted this and saw himself as being like one of these Ubermensch, and someone who could commit atrocities against lesser races. He mixed up a cocktail of lies that ended in the Holocaust, the Nazi genocide of the Jews. However, Nietzsche's work was also part of the background for artists and society revaluing the tribal art of "natural savages" and "primitive" peoples as an antidote to strict rationality and uninspired, civil society. Expressionism, as a means to truth, became highly valued again, as Schelling's aesthetic philosophy, rather than Hegel's respected rationality, became the main cultural influence.

CUBISM + FUTURISM

Pablo Picasso joined symbolism and analytics in the way that he combined the abstract and the figurative in his paintings. In 1906, he painted oversized nude women, and monumental sculptural figures that recalled Paul Gauguin's primitive art, Cezanne's multiple perspectives and African tribal masks. And this led directly to "Les Demoiselles d'Avignon" in 1907. This shows three naked ladies whose angular faces have been copied from African tribal masks. Picasso used these because of their essence, their wild energy. His new system of Cubist painting did a violence to traditional art by the way it analysed and abstracted objects into different elements and different viewpoints, then put them all back together in one work. It encapsulated the dynamism of the age, reconfiguring the wild energy into a new, analytical way of looking at beauty and painting (A2 and B2 in our schema).

This style was then developed into a more expressive direction by the Italian Futurists e.g. Giacomo Balla, Umberto Boccioni and Gino Severini, and a more modern, symbolic direction by the British

Vorticists e.g. Wyndham Lewis, all of whose art celebrated the power and dynamism of the age of the machine. These abstract avant-garde artists expressed the practical and political effects of by technology and mechanisation. And this differed to Picasso's later, formal portrait and still life exercises and to Cezanne's almost scientific abstraction of nature.

The belief in the formal, analytical, abstract powers of Modernism and Modern art led to a rejection of works that were expressive of the powers of nature (Cezanne, Gaugin, van Gogh) and went further than the formal art exercises of the Cubists or the naïve celebration of technology of the Futurists. It led to the works of the political and mystical artists who preferred systems of abstract thought, more akin to Hegel's dialectical system that to Schelling's philosophy.

ABSTRACT

Artists began to create work that was completely abstract. These Avant-Garde artists, like Piet Mondrian and Wassily Kandinsky, were influenced by Communism and by Theosophy (a Western form of Hindu and Buddhist mysticism). Both systems had a belief in universal ideas and their complete abstraction directly manifested their political and the mystical ideas (A1 in our religious art classification). And these Communist and mystical artists were linked through Hegel.

John Golding, painter, curator and art historian, argues that Mondrian is just one of many artists influenced by Hegel's dialectic and by Madame Helena Petrovna Blavatsky's Theosophical theories (from the late nineteenth century). Theosophical doctrines concerned a united, transcendent consciousness that occurs through the balancing of opposites in a continual process of evolution. And Taylor thinks that this is as if Hegel's ideas were put into a populist spiritual context (10).

Flat, abstract art is seen as being more truthful than an illusion of perspective on a painted surface, so flatness can be used in order to bring spiritual truth near to the viewer. As a result Mondrian intends his painting's surface to become the whole image – and not to just contain representations within the painting's surface (11), e.g.

"Composition with Yellow, Red, Black, Blue and Grey", oil on canvas, 1920. Colour theory was also a strong element in Theosophy and in Mondrian's work. So the arrangements of areas of colour became vital. Blavatsky's view that fluidity and water are the fundamental reality also showed in the visual rhythm and dynamism of Mondrian's work (12). These designs also extend beyond the canvas, linking to infinity.

Other artists and art theorists were influenced by the political philosopher Karl Marx (1818-1883) who developed Hegel's dialectical thinking into a materialistic, secular system. Glenn Ward describes how Marx saw that, in an industrial, Capitalist system, for people to be able to buy commodities, they need to sell their labour and become a commodity themselves. The workers are alienated from the objects that they produce and each other. Money becomes the new social bond and society is based on "exchange values" rather than "use values". When "exchange value" (money) is less than should be given for the "use value" (work done) exploitation results (13).

Society was seen as having two levels, an "economic base" of commercial realities and a "cultural superstructure" of the entertainment and politics that function on top of this. The superstructure produces goods for people to fill the gap in their lives that the exploitation creates. These goods are designed so that you cannot see that they are created by a system whose inadequacy creates the need for them in the first place. Marx wanted the worker to see this relationship to the capitalist system through a critical analysis so workers could end exploitation and create a united, communist society based on equality.

Russian Artists like Kasimir Malevich linked to Hegel's dialectical system, where in the final stage of evolution, the spirit links to a universal, abstract form (14). This expression of the universal was part of Malevich's Suprematism, a movement that linked to science and geometry. The images were created directly and without self-consciousness or symbolic content. His "White Square on White", oil on canvas 1918, represents a conclusion to the series. In 1919 Malevich then took these images and applied them in a practical way as a revolutionary activist with the communist party, decorating rallies and parades (15). Their purity of thought was symbolic of the workers need for purity of critical analysis.

Golding suggests that Kandinsky sympathised with the Russian Revolution but rejected Marx's materialism for a mystical dimension. Kandinsky, in "Concerning the Spiritual in Art" 1911, says that the images would be read subconsciously and transport the viewer to a higher spiritual realm. He made his work in a semi-trance state and considered that he had achieved a great synthesis, a reconciliation of the unreconcilable, and that the epoch of the Great Spiritual had begun (16).

"Composition VIII", oil on canvas 1923, shows his belief in the circle as a symbol of the synthesis of oppositions. In the work can be traced figurative symbols such as boats and lance bearing horsemen. These were characteristic of earlier works such as "Composition IV", oil on canvas 1911, and show how Kandinsky incorporated abstract mysticism with symbols of Russia and he even used symbols of the Russian Orthodox Church (17).

Another artist, Marc Chagall, worked with the Communist party in 1918 but he conflicted with the purely abstract work of the Suprematists. Monica Bohm-Duchen considered the peeping figures in works like "Profile at Window" 1918, to be ways of slyly subverting the "purity" of Suprematism (18).

His art projects in Soviet Russia included theatre and town decoration and he suggested that people need to live in small communities. Chagall was suspicious of a grand Hegelian synthesis in art and a grand Marxist revolution. Instead he integrated local individuals and humanity with politics and religious tradition.

Chagall joined the everyday with the mystical and, although he was not practicing, his orthodox Jewish upbringing was a constant theme of his work. Whilst Jewish art is seen as non-representational and denies the use of graven images, Chagall thought his Jewish folk art had a tradition of being representational. He also considered his use of folk art as a way to relate to universal concerns. This was in contrast to the impersonal universalism of Modernism or Communism.

Monica Bohm-Duchen states that a continuing theme of Chagall's art was his link in a heaven and earth, man and God. Chagall's early "Homage to Apollinaire" 1911-12 shows Adam and Eve with their two bodies merged in a circle. Bohm-Duchen thinks that this represents a Kabbalistic concern for the joining of duality with unity, abstraction and figuration. This union is also expressed in numerous pictures of romantic love by Chagall (19).

Chagall shows the tension between the abstract work of the avant-garde and his own kitsch and figurative Jewish art for ordinary humanity. There was a clear dialectical split between the totalitarian state and individual expression. After visiting Palestine, and his experiences in Nazi Germany, Chagall developed his Jewish themes. His depictions of the crucified Christ as a Jew e.g. "White Crucifixion" 1938 has figures in mass political movements sweeping as destructive hordes, across the picture. It is, perhaps, a way of noting the irony that the Nazi persecution of the Jews was the same as the Jews persecution of Christ. This Nazi persecution ended in the Holocaust and changed the face of Western art.

Another artist who expressed the concerns of individual suffering within a religious tradition and Communism was Frida Kahlo. Her surreal paintings were emblems of her suffering. They are symbolic and represent loss of innocence through violence (physical and sexual) perpetrated on women by men. Kahlo was a Communist and whilst her paintings contain elements of macabre Mexican Christian religious paintings this is part of a psychological understanding of the history of suffering of women. The works are representational e.g. "The Two Fridas" 1939 where two version of the artists sit together, one in white (who has cut out her own heart) and one in blue who has the heart placed upon her chest. Behind them are storm clouds. However, the suffering of women artists, and the influence of state institutions upon this, would not really be broadly evaluated until the 1960's.

Early Communist abstraction had helped define what was Modern art whilst artists like Chagall and Kahlo helped create something more human. The abstract art had not found mass appeal in Soviet Russia. As a result Stalin's kitsch Social Realist propaganda was used to try and inspire workers so that Stalin's government could achieve social control. This kind or Social Realist work became associated with what was not art. It began to arise in Europe along with the evils of Modernist totalitarianism (both Communist and Fascist).

FIGURATIVE KITSCH

The Nazis, also preferred traditional, figurative, narrative art forms that celebrated human ideals (A2) and rejected abstract Modern art. Ironically, Mystical Theosophy was adopted by both Nazis and the Avant-garde. The Avant-garde aimed at a universal energy and an international unity, whilst Nazism directed its energy to national goals.

The Nazis rejected strict universalism and materialism in favour of racial purity and spiritual destiny. Using Darwin's idea of the survival of the fittest they combined their genetic and eugenic theories with their aim to create a Thousand Year Reich to defend the Aryan race against Communism and Jewish Modernism. Christ was seen as an Aryan from Thule, in the North, one of a pure race of "Supermen." Aryan Masters who would lead the herd in the "Thousand Year Reich" against the Bolshevik Jews, the cosmic enemy. Idealised images of the German people were used in Nazi propaganda to further this aim.

Marx, Freud and Einstein were Jewish, as were many artists and art collectors and financiers. And the Nazis were against the cultural values of Modernism. Hitler viewed the art of the Jewish Modernists as being degenerate and against beauty. He saw them as unskilled and worthless art criminals and their Jewish press, with its so-called art criticism, as full of mendacious claptrap and jabbering. For him true German Art, of heroes and landscapes, expressed the essence of the German people.

Hitler had been an artist selling scenes of Germany and he believed that Jews had rejected him from the Academy of Fine Arts because he did not follow their degenerate expressionism and surrealism. He later saw his political rallies in Nuremburg as theatre like Wagnerian opera.

Clement Greenberg argued, in his influential 1939 essay "Avant-Garde and Kitsch", that the Avant-Garde was needed to stop culture going into the hands of capitalism and fascism. He argued that the avant-garde was concerned with innovation and progress but fascist countries used kitsch in order to keep them connected with the masses and as a way to revere past-masters and historical culture. Greenberg saw mass produced advertising and imagery as kitsch that was produced to directly appeal to popular taste. Kitsch was seen as being valued because it is easily recognised, provides a story and exaggerates reality (20). It takes the forms of high culture yet is mechanically reproduced and is spurious.

Greenberg suggests that true socialism gives the right conditions for education so that people can appreciate true (i.e. avant-garde and abstract) culture (21). He argued that beauty in art is in an understanding of the object. Painting was an investigation of the formal properties of paint on a canvas and the property that was particular to the medium was flatness and abstraction was part of this flatness (22).

Greenberg's ideas developed out of Modernist political anaylysis (Critical Thinking). This thinking was created by using Karl Marx's theories into an analysis of an oppressive "cultural superstructure" and how mass media images were used in this. The line of thinking was developed by Theodor Adorno, Max Horkheimer, Walter Benjamin, Greenberg and later by Guy Debord. In his paper for the 1985 ICA conference on postmodernism Michael Newman in describes how Adorno and Horkheimer's adapted Marx to argue that kitsch is linked with a culture industry that is debased and popular and leads away from real experience and social community (23).

Initially they saw the potentially positive effects of the mass media on the critical thinking of the public, but this soon turned to seeing the negative effect of its complete pacifying of the political imagination and ability to see reality. It completely engulfs the individual in an inescapable viewpoint that separates them from political reality by an alienating superstructure.

In "The Work of Art in the age of Mechanical Reproduction" 1936, Walter Benjamin optimistically argued that technologies of mass production could make art equally available to everyone. Older works of art often had special powers because of their use within oppressive religious cults and ceremonies and Benjamin thought it was good to strip away that aura and allow open access to all people (24) The "aura" of exclusivity of original works could be stripped away by making mass copies. Cinema in particular was an example of a mass art that did not even have a single, original copy. However he was unsure that this would be responsibly handled. The problem for him was that mass production gave more items at a faster rate and thus it was hard to be critical about all of these. Production, without critical thought allows exploitative politics to be promoted and glorified (25) i.e. at the time this theorising occurred there were fascist mass spectacles and an increasingly commercialised mass culture and the use of social realism by Soviet Communists.

To counter these concerns we see how Susan Buck-Morss, in "Dream World of Mass Culture", says that Benjamin proposed that the images produced by consumer society have a limited life (and are continually replaced by newer fashions and images) and that this constant change opens up the possibility of a radical reconstruction of the fragmented reality of industrial society. Such reconstruction is possible because the need for it lies at an unconscious, mythic, level in human beings. (26) Benjamin states that people can be awakened and made aware of their concrete historical situation (27). One of the ways in which they thought that this could be done was through the new abstract art and that understanding such art helps politically empower people to be critical about the dialectical ideology of progress.

Whilst Benjamin thought that mass culture had a critical potential ten years later Theodor Adorno and Max Horkheimer, in "The Culture Industry" 1945, described mass culture as cheap parody reproduced by technology. And that the makers of low culture e.g. the cinema, create individual consumers who seek identity by imitating manufactured capitalist stars and use humour to promote the viewer's resignation to oppressed conditions. Thus, only dialectical, critical, thinking can give alternatives to popular culture and people should not be influenced by popular culture (28).

DADA SURREALISM

Chagall and Kahlo had been exploring ways of symbolic social comment that was not just Social Realism and that employed art styles to convey a more personal message. Picasso had also done this in works like "Guernica" 1937.

In 1937 Nazi planes rained incendiary bombs on the Basque town of Guernica to aid the fascist General Franco in the Spanish Civil War. This murder of 1,600 civilians was the first ever deliberate bombing of civilians. Picasso put aside his still lives and nudes and made "Guernica", in 6 weeks, as a response to the outrage. It was a reaction against fascism and the artwork was sent, touring Europe and America to raise funds for the Republicans. It is an 8 metre wide and 3 metre high painting that is a riot of twisted limbs, screaming men reaching up and mothers grieving for dead babies. A horse writhes and a bull is in vicious panic. All are reduced to abstract shapes that are in the fitting form of modern fragmentation, a shrapnel of death and destruction.

Picasso rejected the two extremes of complete abstraction and anthropomorphic representation and this had also been rejected by the Surrealists, although Surrealism also has two art forms, both of which were political. Left wing, Avant-garde Surrealism deconstructed figurative symbols into abstraction, e.g. Dadaism. Right wing Surrealism constructed figurative symbols out of the unconscious, e.g. Dali's Surrealism. Both forms rejected the analytical thought of the Cubists and abstract artists and of Modernity (whilst paradoxically still remaining within Modernity).

Dadaism broke down everyday structures and figures into subconscious and abstract combinations. The link of art to the everyday was introduced when Marcel Duchamp made ordinary objects into art, these objects were termed "readymades" or "found art". His most famous work "Fountain" 1917 is a urinal that he signed R.Mutt. This broke down the idea that only paintings could be art but also reinforce that the artist could magically transform substances. It was the beginning of the importance of concepts and conceptual art. It also began a move towards scatological (the study of filth) and formless art which we shall look at in due course along with its profound influence on Modern art.

Another method of Dada art was automatic drawing which was to be developed later by the Abstract Expressionists who we shall also look at after looking at Salvador Dali, an artist who focussed on a more on kitsch version of Surrealism and who was linked to Franco.

Fiona Bradley, a curator at the Tate Gallery, argues in her 1998 Dali exhibition catalogue, that Dali made his own mythic structures and using traditional images with new and unusual meanings. She suggests Dali had a desire for mystical resolution An example of his mysticism is "The Madonna of Port Lligat" (first version) 1949. Here the Madonna and the classical structure are split and Bradley thinks that this refers to the splitting of the atom and relates to the power of the eternal, mystical feminine. The model used in the portrait is Dali's wife, who Dali also saw as his complementary opposite and his link to the eternal feminine. She is the Virgin Mother, beyond rational man, and the female form is a conduit through which this energy can reach us, via the birth of the son (29).

I suggest that the ultimate aim of his work is religious, e.g. "Perpignan Railway Station" 1965, inspired by what Dali, in his Diary of a Genius, called his "cosmoginic ecstasy" - an exact vision of the constitution of the Universe, which was similar in structure to the Perpignan railway station (30). At the centre of the picture, Dali's image is superimposed on to Christ and God's rays of light. The painting incorporates the praying figures of a painting by Jean-Francois Millet "The Angelus" 1858-9 where the couple are repenting after having illicit sex. Dali's painting creates comical images of their sexual encounter on the wheel-barrow, shown in The Angelus (31).

Bradley says this work presents an oedipal myth by which Dali could interpret his life. The male is father, son and Dali and the female is daughter, mother and Dali's wife Gala. I think that Dali posits the resolution of sexual conflicts in a father figure that cannot be overturned i.e. God and Dali. It is not in a mystical union with the mother as Bradley suggests. Rather it refers to the relationship between God the Father and the Incarnate Son, who destroys the

Father (himself). This is like the Freudian Tribal view where the dominant male (Father) is sacrificed by the Tribe (Son) to be consumed and replaced with a new Tribal leader. It is an example of the artist arrogantly becoming like God, like a Pharaoh or a Fuhrer.

ABSTRACT EXPRESSIONISM

This kind of symbolism of Dali's relates to dynamics of domination and much religious art also comes in a mass produced kitsch form and so is also a form of alienating, dominating culture industry. Prior to the Second World War there was a Modernist rejection of faith in God but after the war (with the Nazi Holocaust, Soviet genocides and the use of bombs in Hiroshima and Nagasaki) there was a renewed crisis in faith in God but now this was coupled with a new crisis of faith in Modernism's Grand Narratives of progress through science and technology. Fascist narrative kitsch was rejected in favour of abstraction that expressed the new nihilism and existential anxiety about the Modern age.

Narrative was removed by Modern abstract artists and Golding notes (32) that whilst the Europeans painted intellectual abstraction, the Americans became their abstract art/canvas through expression. They painted in a style that came to be referred as Abstract Expressionism or Action painting, also known as the New York School.

Golding suggests that Jackson Pollock's "Male and Female in Search of a Symbol", oil on canvas, 1943 shows his desire to reconcile opposites in a symbolic language. Pollock was influenced by Jungian psychology, by Jung's symbolic systems and by the idea of the individual delving into their own unconscious (33) to find psychological unity. Using the symbols of American Indian tribal art, shamanism and ritual magic, he tried to link man and the eternal in his art. Golding says that this contrasts with the Freudian, sexual focus of Surrealists like Salvador Dali (34).

His work developed out of the earlier Surrealist technique of automatic drawing where the artist closed down his conscious mind so that he could express himself directly from his unconscious mind. Pollock painted as if possessed, making short, rhythmic strokes and the very action of art producing was seen as a way of shamanistic healing or salvation. By 1947 his symbolic imagery was replaced by pure energy/action and the gesture itself, e.g. "Full Fathom Five", oil on canvas, 1947. The work was made of short, rhythmic strokes that cancel each other in the overall surge of the painting (35). It is a piece of improvised jazz music to be listened to, rather than a story to be understood. Another example is a 1.5 metre wide, 1 metre high painting. "Number 3, 1949: Tiger", where the complex interweaving and interlacing layers of primary coloured paint form a battleground. Yet the colours balance each other and are held together with black lines that work like rigid markers.

B.H. Friedman quotes Pollock's journals in "Jackson Pollock, Energy Made Visible", London, 1972 with Pollock saying that his concern is with the rhythms of nature (like Mondrian) and that he doesn't copy objects from nature as he thought "I am nature" because his gestures of pure energy connected to the very forces of nature locked in his unconscious mind. The viewer standing before the work is then directly confronted by forces of nature (36).

But not only Jackson Pollock's brutal canvasses, with their splashed in red and black gouges of paint, helped make Pollock famous. Along with the Museum of Modern Art promoting his art, the C.I.A. also promoted his abstract art because it helped us in the "Cold War" as his expressions of freedom and individualism were opposite to Soviet "Social Realist" art, with all its kitsch pictures of workers and party leaders. This support by the capitalist state was ironic as Greenberg had supported the work for being Avant-garde.

But the real mystic was Mark Rothko who engulfed his viewers in dark, profound colour paintings e.g. "No.10", 1950, Oil on canvas, 1950. His large, vertical, rectangular paintings are dabbed and daubed in two main blocks of colour that are like clouds, floating as a heavenly doorway. These doorways through the infinite, have a dividing line that is like the horizon point of a landscape. It is as if Friedrich's Wanderer has entered into the Sublime Sea of Fog. Rothko sought an unfettered expression of his Jewish mysticism. But it was tinged with the despair of the Second World War, the gas chambers, the atomic bomb. Mankind had sunk into a new barbarism and it was out of this despair that Rothko tried to transport himself into a sublime, a pure experience of truth.

The viewer can merge with these sublime landscapes. However, his doorways were clouded, more like expressions of despair. It is as if he had been making money with a style that worked, with doorways that he never passed through, to complete his vision of mystical union. And he suffered a long period of depression that ended in suicide.

Rothko was influenced by the Qabbalah (Jewish mysticism) as was Barnett Newman whose "Onement I", oil on canvas 1948, relates to the twelfth century Qabbalistic text the Zohar, which describes the unity of male and female principles, from which the divine light emanated.

In his essay "The Sublime is Now" 1948 in Tiger's Eye, December 1948, Newman argues for a rejection of beauty as primary and a return to a sense of the sublime. Newman argued that for Kant the apprehension of beauty was more associated with concepts of morality than the thrill of sublimity. For Newman the new abstract art was like a sublime doorway to an aesthetic absolute that transcended Kant's categories of understanding (37).

The Modernists, like the Greeks, believed in progress through reason and the arts. The Modernists used reason to kill faith in God and now needed art to fill the void, so they sought Enlightenment in abstract art like Pollock, Rothko and Newman's.

Pollock's abstract expressionism was akin to the Avant Garde desire to break down capitalist structure and to give a pure abstract art, however, the work no longer had an Avant-garde political effect and was too abstract for the majority of people. Instead he became an art celebrity within a consumerist art structure that was used politically against Communist, Stalinist, "Social Realist" art). Rothko continued with Pollock' venture but his work marked the continued failure to be able to reach the mystical through their artistic venture whilst within a consumer society.

Then Abstract Expressionists began to create forms out of their Formless void and this marked the beginning of the complete integration with the commercial world.

Willem de Kooning had painted women regularly in the early 1940s and his early abstractions were derived from objects found in the studio. In the 1950's he began to explore the subject of women exclusively. "Woman V" (1952–53) was one of many on this theme. He used heightened colours and lines in works that were both representational and geometricized. Figures would overlap other figures which in turn might be overlapped by dripping lines of paint thus playing with space.

The works caused a sensation because they were figurative, not abstract like the work of his fellow painters, and they were also Abstract Expressionists because of their aggressive brushwork and bright, saturated colours used. His images also linked to the primitive immediacy of the Abstract Expressionist painting process. They were of snarling, powerful women with huge breasts and enlarged eyes. These were from the unconscious and linked to some of modern man's deepest sexual fears of being devoured by the feminine (and to the death of the male ego in the mystical, universal, feminine consciousness).

At a similar time, in England, Francis Bacon, a figurative painter, became known for his bold and emotionally raw imagery. He expressed a dark existentialist outlook on life through his paintings of objects within abstract environments, e.g. in his 1944 triptych "Three Studies for Figures at the Base of a Crucifixion". Here biomorphic forms twist around in agony in a deep red space. This work showed Bacon to be a bleak, prophet of the human condition creating environments where people are harmed whilst other people watch.

Bacon also used religious imagery of the crucifixion to examine dark areas of human behaviour. His "Study after Velázquez's Portrait of Pope Innocent X" (1953) is another example of his works where semi abstract figures torturously scream or writhe in geometrical cages set against flat, nondescript backgrounds.

The new art forms being created were both violent, misogynistic (de Kooning) and anti-religious (Bacon). They marked a reformation out of an abstract energy into a dark picture of human nature. An acceptance of the horrific nature of this world brought with it the desire for escape and for the majority of people this was through a post-war consumer heaven was created. But for artists it was through a further breakdown that they would be led to Gnostic mysticism.

CARNIVAL AND FORMLESS

Both abstract and realist art can be seen as positive and constructive but Modern art also had a negative role. The positive role, seen in artists like Kandinsky, Mondrian and Rothko, was to erect new aesthetic structures. The negative role, seen in Dadaism, was to break down structures, and this was part of an ongoing political fight against the totalitarian structures of Fascism, Communism and consumerism. And this Dadaist breakdown eventually became a mystical ideology.

The influential Soviet philosopher Mikhael Bakhtin reacted against any kind of intellectual or moral stasis and neatly ordered "logical" systems." He was anti-Stalinist and he used the idea of the Mediaeval Carnival to break down social oppression through "reverse hierarchy," which is a "humbling, debunking, or debasing" "and a lowering of all forms of expression in language or art." (38)

Clark & Holquist say that Bakhtin's notion of a carnival world is "organized horizontally rather than vertically." "all are considered equal and brotherhood is universal." "Everything is constantly moving and changing." The celebrations are a release from oppressive authority. And "the body emphasises changes in its nature through eating, evacuation, or sex, as opposed to the static ideal represented in classical Greek marbles, is "grotesque". The grotesque body is flesh as the site of becoming."

Using laughter and everyday words in language was a way to bring down authority. And it was still seen as a way to challenge the culture industry. This Carnival and the grotesque breaks down the ideal into the bodily and the horizontal and this has parallels in the notion of the Formless.

In "Formless – A Users Guide" Yve-Alain Bois and Rosalind Krauss say that the term "informe" comes from Georges Bataille and that "informe, (*is*) a de-classing in every sense of the term:" (8) This de-classing was a breaking down of hierarchies of form and matter to produce an entropy, a homogenized, horizontal levelling that is a way "of liberating our thinking from the semantic, the servitude to thematics," (9) In other words it is a rejection of high ideals and oppressive systems by using the lowest and most accessible materials.

Bois and Krauss (39) give four operations of the formless; horizontality, base materialism, entropy and pulsation.

Horizontality is in the levelling of all attempts at vertical power structures like language, for example, "the article Leiris devotes to spit makes the desublimatory nature of the dictionary clear:" (40) This is part of a sabotage of academic systems, by appearing to be one whilst being incomplete and non-alphabetical.

The formless breaks down structure in art production into its base material nature: "the concept of image presupposes a possible distinction between form and matter, and it is this distinction, insofar as it is an abstraction, that the operation of the formless tries to collapse". (41)

Matter and form are reduced to a formless entropy and a stasis: "But Bataille's fascination with rot and waste, with the decomposition of everything, which finds expression in almost every one of his texts, shows well enough that the entropic freeze, whether or not he wanted to keep it at bay in his writing, was an essential operation for him,". (42)

Despite this stasis a basic pulsating energy is left. This pulsation echoes the sexual and gives a bodily emphasis that we are enticed to become involved in. It breaks down the idealised as it "involves an endless beat that punctures the disembodied self-closure of pure visuality and incites an irruption of the carnal." (43)

THE THEATRE OF ARTAUD

An artist whose work expressed this tendency to the formless is Piero Manzoni. His "Merda D'artista" 1961 is a series of tins of the artist's own excrement. However, the essence of the formless is not to be taken so literally in art. More important is the breakdown of high structures (e.g. political, aesthetic, epistemological, scientific) that is the operation of the formless. This breakdown can be seen in the Surrealist Anton Artaud's "Theatre of Cruelty" where he used theatre, music, cinema and carnival circus. Artaud aimed to break down structures as a method to reach a mystical dimension.

Jane Goodall in "Artaud and the Gnostic Drama" argues that Artaud was influenced by the Gnostic idea of God as the Demi-urge who imposes an evil masculine order onto feminine matter. In Artaud's second letter of his "Letters of Cruelty" he considers the world to be naturally evil and that the creation of goodness has to be desired and willed. This creative action, however, creates more evil despite the will for creating goodness (44). This seeming paradox can be explained because the Gnostic's world is immanent and fallen. As a result all created goodness is just part of a fallen nature and cannot be truly good. True goodness is achieved only in transcending the immanent world.

Artaud hoped to go beyond everyday life by using shocking imagery and sounds to "cruelly" question the beliefs and expectations of the audience. He used repetition and a tight script (as a form of mantra or Zen koan) and meditational breathing and actions "throwing the audience into a magical trance" is via "pressure points" that "must be affected in the body." (45).

In his article "An Affective Athleticism" he posits that inhaling is a masculine, creative act and exhaling is a feminine dying. We achieve a balance between the two in a sacred breathing. This breathing overcomes the cycle of opposites of life and death in a transcendent (seventh breath) state. "And a seventh state higher than breathing, uniting the revealed and the unrevealed through the portals of a higher Guna, the state of Sattva." (46) This "Sattva" is beyond opposites (dualities) and is mystical. As such Artaud's work is akin to the Tantric rites used to shock and jolt people into a state of Enlightened, mystical awareness.

Goodall contrasts Nietzsche's and Artaud's views of God to show how the Western and the Gnostic, mystical perspectives differ. For Nietzsche destiny belongs to the individual, rather than God, and Nietzsche uses a Western philosophical system, based on language, dialectic and conceptual oppositions. In contrast Artaud's Theatre threatens theology and spoken language (logos). For Nietzsche and Artaud God enslaves us through language (47). For Nietzsche the release from God's or language's control is through Dionysian dance and music. For Artaud release is through "total theatre". This kind of Gnostic ritual is a blend of A1 and B1 on the schema.

Nietzsche leaves rational structures in place whilst Artaud breaks these down. Artaud calls us to throw off this God who leads us only into matter and away from our true self. The self needs reconstructing by violently rejecting the Laws of God (48).

Nietzsche's God is philosophical and the concept of him stops men asking authentic questions for themselves. In contrast Artaud sees that even the questions themselves need rejecting. The original cosmic presence is prior to language. Language creates the notion of a self and the thought of "I" causes the real self to disappear. Artaud is not just against language but against the body and the created world itself. As a result "Artaud equates creation with cruelty and proposes to undertake the work of counter-cruelty in his theatre".

Goodall says (49) that Susan Sontag says that Gnosticism is the attempt to free the spirit from a world where matter is vile and the spirit is in conflict with the body. Sontag criticises Gnosticism and Artuad, saying that this position does not create a political revolution, only a personal one. However, Sontag misses the point that Artaud's work is a rejection of political processes which are worldly and fallen.

Artaud is not seeking an endpoint that mankind aims for and he does not posit an origination point. Goodall (50) quotes the philosopher Jacques Derrida's "Writing and Difference", 183 saying that Artaud's art is without works. This is because Artaud is fighting against the notion of a creator God/demi-urge: "by crediting him with an art without works. Derrida refuses Artaud the status of creator, which is his most complex, persistent, and impassioned claim against the demiurgical imposition of constituted being."

Artaud saw theatre as illusory and divisive, but he also saw life as illusory and divisive: "What could prevent me believing in the illusion of theatre since I believe in the illusion of reality?" (51).

Baker-White says that Derrida recognises the paradoxical impossibility of Artaud's task. That Derrida thinks the "Theatre of Cruelty" inhabited, rather than produced, non-theological space, free from the mediated process of representation and the model of this was communal festival (52).

Artuad's work is a rejection of a world created by a "philosophical", logos based Demiurge. His solution is to use contradiction to paralyse rationality and thus transcend contradiction so that the performers and the audience, realise that they are identical to the essence of the universe.

A number of artists in the 1960's and 70's began using Artaudian themes. Performance artists also became like priests of new religions, e.g. Hermann Nitsch's Dionysian animal sacrifices were performance pieces, that involved controlled violence and mutilation. In the 1950s, Nitsch conceived of the Orgien Mysterien Theater staging nearly 100 performances between 1962 and 1998. His work was both ritualistic and existential and includes slaughtered, skinned, mutilated and crucified animals. Nitsch's work also incorporated music, dancing, audience participation and quasi-religious icons. This work questions the sacrificial origins and moral basis of religion. But is also a shock from religious thinking.

The German performance artist who developed this quasi-religious direction into a more celebrity role was Joseph Beuys. In 1944 Beuys's plane was shot down on the Crimean Front and he claimed that he was rescued from the crash by Tatar tribesmen, who wrapped his broken body in animal fat and felt and nursed him back to health. Later, in 1962, Beuys began a brief formal involvement with Fluxus, a loose international group of artists who championed a radical erosion of the boundaries of art, bringing creative practice into the everyday.

Although Fluxus was inspired by the Dada Surrealists, Beuys thought that Duchamp and his idea of the Readymade (and the breakdown of art/social structures) was overrated. As such Beuys is more in the tradition of Dali than Duchamp. Dali took on a semi-divine persona of a genius in his symbolic surrealism and Beuys produced symbolic ritualistic performances and developed the persona of a Shaman (a tribal priest in Animistic religions). This was a full taking on of an identity as if to enable himself and the viewer passage between different physical and spiritual states.

His work is also grounded in humanism, social philosophy and Anthroposophy (a movement allied with mystical Theosophy and with an emphasis on colour, movement and dance). Beuys however, became an individual art personality with his symbolic, animistic, mythology (rather than breaking down of structures to facilitate an Artaudian mystical consciousness).

In "I Like America and America Likes Me" (1974) New York, Beuys shared the René Block Gallery with a wild coyote, for eight hours over three days. He stood, wrapped in a thick, grey blanket of felt, leaning on a large shepherd's staff. He lay on the straw, as the coyote watched him, or shredded the blanket to pieces. At the end of the three days, Beuys hugged the coyote that had grown tolerant of him, and was taken to the airport. He wanted to insulate himself and see nothing of America other than the coyote.

Benjamin Buchloh criticizes Beuys for not appreciating the consequences of the work of Duchamp, that institutions create meaning for art objects (hence Duchamp was able to make a urinal into a work of art). For Buchloh, Beuys tried to control the meanings of his art, in esoteric or symbolic codings, rather than acknowledging the art museum and dealership formation of meaning. (53)

During the 1960s Beuys formulated his concept of social sculpture, motivated by a utopian belief in the power of universal human creativity and revolutionary change. The idea is that society as a whole is one great work of art (with echoes of the Wagnerian Gesamtkunstwerk (total artwork) that also influenced Hitler) to which each person can contribute creatively.

An example of this idea in practice is his 1982 work for Documenta 7, which was a large pile of stones making an arrow pointing to an oak tree that he had planted. A tree had to be planted in the location of each stone with each tree as a living monument contrasting with the unmoving stone that it was planted next to. So 7,000 oak trees were then planted in Kassel, Germany as a participatory social sculpture and Beuys's wanted people to create environmental and social change through this project. However, again for Buchloh, art's power for political transformation is limited by the aspirations of the art museum and dealership networks and so Beuys' social art is limited in what it achieves.

SITUATIONISM AND SOCIETY OF THE SPECTACLE

Artists had earlier rejected the authoritarian governments but were also aware that they could not escape corporate control, and that all of culture had become a series of brand names, images and thought patterns to trap people as impotent consumers.

The danger of social control through using shallow imagery, was theorized by Guy Debord in an idea called the Spectacle. The Spectacle is an ensemble of independent, commodity representations that the spectator is separate and isolated from. In "The Society of the Spectacle" 1967 Debord argued that the economy of late 20th century society is driven by images as production and consumption of commodities is so prevalent that life is now even lived around images of these commodities. We watch our experiences and relationships rather than have them for ourselves and become apathetic about thinking that we can change how we should feel. The Spectacular society denies a view of history as being part of a dialectical progression (54). Debord thinks that opposition to the Spectacle is by dialectical (critical) thinking and by having personal relations based around direct communication between people, not consumer activities (55). The "Situationist International" movement arose out of this opposition to the Spectacle and members tried to create events and experiences that broke out of packaged and commodified ways of thinking.

I think that the ability to overcome this kind of amnesia that was explored by Walter Benjamin in "Dream World of Mass Culture" Susan Buck-Morss says that Benjamin proposed that the world of images produced by consumer society has a limited life and is continually replaced by newer fashions and images. This change opens up the possibility of radical change that lies at an unconscious, mythic, level in human beings. This mythic change would not be to return to a (pre-industrial) nature but to a radical reconstruction of the fragmented reality of industrial society, (56) not through artistic individualism but through collective revolutionary energy. (57)

In "Dream City and Dream House, Dreams of the Future, Anthropological Nihilism, Jung" Benjamin (58) states that the waking being is aware of its concrete historical situation by placing itself in a politically empowered, critical, dialectical ideology of progress. Thus the use of shock and the breaking of convention can awaken people to their sleeping political condition and give them the chance to begin Critical Thinking.

This escape resembles a Gnostic release from a consumer society that resembles a fallen world created by the Demi-urge who had trapped human souls. However, whilst Gnostics like Artaud wanted to paralyse rationality, other thinkers, like Benjamin, saw art as a way to help people think clearly i.e. critically, historically and politically. Although both wanted to challenge the system.

By the 1960s artists had begun to challenge the hard, geometric, abstract art in galleries which were also associated with oppressive, male institutions (and were no longer seen as Avant-garde and revolutionary). Civil, racial, gay and women's rights movements became the subject of art and this was the beginnings of the art of identity politics. The expressive Dionysian was embraced as a means to achieve this and religion was still rejected as part of the problem of male hierarchy.

Henry Sayre notes how, in 1967, Michael Fried argued in his influential essay "Art and Objecthood" that Modern, abstract art should be autonomous, continually present and outside time and history, whereas the Minimalists had a theatrical relationship to the art object where the object was part of an environment that was related to (59). Newman suggests that the minimal object was process based, rather than being a fixed product, as the viewer's relation to the work was part of the work itself (60).

These debates had become purely aesthetic and without political or spiritual direction. The abstract purity of work like Dan Flavin's neon tube sculptures may have owed something to US Protestant Christianity but this was not a direct influence. Flavin used coloured blocks of yellow, blue and pink in order to bathe architectural areas of the interior of Santa Maria Annunciata in Chiesa Rossa, Milan, 2006. Flavin had worked in mocking the passion of St Theresa in 1963 by using a candy-coloured strip light as a statement of hard Modernity. He used limited light to celebrate a barren room and rejected ideas of spirituality and hidden psychology in his work. He preferred rational simplicity, devoid of meaning and mystery. He said that his art "is what it is and it ain't nothing else."

This shows the contrast in three ways of viewing abstract art, between hard materialistic atheism, mysticism and the churches commissioning of such work as a form of Protestant spiritual (non-figurative/ iconoclastic) design.

Related to Minimalism was Conceptualism and Conceptual art which rejected the commodification of the art market and opened up new lines of enquiry and engagement by returning to Dada style social action. It used temporary, cheap, invisible or reproducible materials, e.g. kitsch, and critiqued and protested against social and art institutions. Performance was also used, like conceptual art, to counter exploitation of the material, commodified forms of art.

Performers created Messianic like self-sacrifices e.g. during his 1974 performance "Trans-fixed" Chris Burden was nailed to the back of a Volkswagen which was driven out of a driveway onto a road. Burden described the marks left by the nails in his hands as stigmata, like the marks that miraculously appear on the hands and feet of Catholic saints in sympathy with the bleeding of Christ:

"Inside a small garage in Speedway Avenue, I stood on the rear bumper of a Volkswagen. I lay on my back over the rear section of the car, stretching my arms onto the roof. Nails were driven through my palms into the roof of the car. The garage door was opening and the car pushed halfway out into Speedway. Screaming for me, the engine was run at full speed for two minutes. After 2 minutes, the engine was turned off and the car pushed back into the garage. The door was closed." (61)

The avant-garde, collaborative, multimedia, performance of the 70s contrasted to "high" abstract Modernism, but this work also related back to the Modernist performance of Futurism and Dadaism. So these were not yet postmodern, even thought they rejected abstract Modernism. Rather it related to the early Modernist avant-garde.

Feminist art used the human body, domesticity and performance as a contrast to the masculine, Modernist institution with its abstract, gallery object. Process based happenings and environments were an Avant-Garde breaking down of male structures. Women formed their own art-forms but these were also used by male artists who gained the recognition from the institutions.

In "Performance: Live Art Since the 60's", RoseLee Goldberg states: "it would take almost thirty years of feminist scholarship to unravel the very different uses of the body by male and female artist of this period, and properly to credit the women artist for their pioneering and highly considered examination of the body as a measure of identity, taboo, and the limits of masculine/feminine emancipation, their belief in the body as prime, raw material, opened numerous territories for artistic investigation." (62)

However, although performance began as political or feminist protest in the 60's it was commodified into scripts, recordings and photographs for galleries (63).

The Guerrilla Girls are artists who have made work since 1985 about the sexism in the New York art scene. They made a poster where they put a gorilla mask onto the head of a bather in the artist Ingre's famous "Grand Odalesque" and posed the question "Do women have to be naked to get into the Metropolitan Museum? Less than 5 per cent of the artists in the Modern Art section are women, but 85 percent of the nudes are female." They had detractors and supporters but to maintain their art careers they had to wear disguises. 20 years later the group had split into different factions and now their work is accepted but the victories of protest art were hard won and the gender imbalance is still large.

In her introduction to art history Cynthia Freeland says that a rejection of politically ineffectual art also led to a re-evaluation of tribal and religious cultures. However, these Indigenous cultures have also been affected by contact with Western techniques of production (64). Freeland describes "primitive", "authentic" and "exotic" cultures as religions under the condition of Late Modernity, i.e. they have become affected by the commodity system.

Freeland describes an exhibition in 1989 called "Les Magiciens de la Terre" at the Pompidous Centre for Modern Art where the earthworks installation piece ,"Red Earth Circle," by Richard Long was exhibited above an earth painting by a collective of Yuendumu Aborigine artist. Freeland says "It is hard to deny that there is a hint of New Age spiritualism in the show's title, which smacks of the desire for "authentic" spirituality and shamanistic authority, to escape participation in a crass and demeaning art market system." (65)

Another aspect of Spiritual work that fits with a desire to escape consumer society is the work of Land and Environmental artists. These works place human creations in nature but in a way that harmonises with the Sublime grandeur of nature. As a result many of the works are on a large scale. These works are then documented in photographs. An example is Richard Long with his work "A Line in Scotland" 1981 (a line of standing stones on a mountain top) and "A Circle in Alaska" 1977 (a flat circle filled with logs, on a beach by the sea). Other proponents include Andy Goldsworthy.

I argue that this environmental work comes from a materialistic atheism for some artists and also from a "New Age" spirituality for other artists. Both are essentially Modernist and the "New Age" spirituality is a unity resembling Schelling's intellectual intuition where religions are united in a common mysticism that is seen as their true essence or teaching. However, even this mysticism was turned into a consumer product and group transcendence via commodity became available through the underground use of L.S.D. The Dionysian ecstasy and Artaudian Gnosis were available to buy in tablet form. With this arose Op art, e.g. the geometrical optical illusions of Bridget Riley, and Psychedelic art with its Hindu and Buddhist stylistic influences on music, fashion, design, festivals and happenings (A1 in our religious art classification scheme). This spiritual drug consumerism gave psychological casualties and highlighted the schizophrenic relationship between consumer culture and mystical experience.

This consumer mysticism was ultimately part of the market. An example of this ineffectual work is Yoko Ono's "Declaration of Nutopia" 1973, a signed document made with John Lennon as ambassadors of a conceptual county that is everywhere. The document is stamped with a seal that pictures the seal of utopia playing with a ball. This fun statement, with serious intent, is about the breakdown of boundaries and borders. It fits with the counter-culture and the artistic fashion for the formless but was an empty symbolic gesture.

MY MODERNIST WORK

From 1996-2001 I tried, in exhibitions and art rituals, to express opposite religious and spiritual perspectives in terms of art forms and to synthesise these opposites (A1 and A2 in the schema). This was a conceptual art project, called The Ism (www.theism.co.uk), that I exhibited at 4 solo shows in London, 2000-2001. The opposites of moral and mystical, figurative and abstract, object and environment, were explored. The conclusion was that the individual is fundamentally divided and moves between two consciousnesses (Moral and Mystical). By accepting this division a limited continuity of self hood is given. I viewed this enlightened schizophrenia as theism rather than pantheism which follows a non-dual merging of opposites.

I reconciled the two perspectives in a Hegelian style dialectic by joining sculptures symbolising different religions, with environmental art and interactive computer installations symbolising mystical consciousness. I joined this high art with everyday life in the "Golden Gate Canvas", a piece of performance art where Israeli police forced me to refrain from creating an abstract expressionist canvas at the Golden Gate, Jerusalem (where the Messiah is supposed to arrive) close to midnight on Millennium Eve (1999/2000).

Linking the art forms together symbolically linked the two perspectives both experientially and conceptually. I later used "Art Rituals" 2001 with shrines, clothing, lighting, music, sculptures and computer scanned imagery of my sculptures in this link of the mystical and moral consciousnesses. This also included a key symbol of a rainbow swastika (an ancient mystical symbol) that was revealed to me through abstract expressionist experiments in Holy Sites, culminating in my making a performance at the Golden Gate, Jerusalem.

I also did a number of performances and art works in stone circles in Cumbria to try and unite performance, environments and nature with sculpture, objects and technology. It symbolically united Nietzsche's Dionysian and the Apollonian perspectives.

Nature is Dionysian and mystical. It relates to changing energy and process. It is non-dualistic, holistic, eternal, experiential, feminine, aesthetic and colourful. It relates to nature and is potentiality and the primal matter of the world. It is horizontal, low cultured and domestic. The mystical breaks down the subject-object, audience-performer divisions. Abstract design, music and performance process are an immediate expression of this nature.

Technology is Apollonian and moral. It relates to fixed form and to objects/products. It is dualistic, atomistic, historical, narrative, masculine, conceptual, meaningful and monochromatic. It relates to faith in technology and to free will imposing form on nature. It is vertical, high cultured, political and moral. It also reinforces the subject-object, audience-performer divisions. Figurative art gives representations of this idea of nature.

My "The Ism" project with its art rituals combined all of these elements, however, it became a universalistic union that was more non-dualistic and mystical and without specific religious symbolism. It did not seek an escape from the commodity system, however, it was a new dialogue for art, that put religion as more important than art whilst exploring the relationships between religion, spirituality and art. And as such it progressed a critical understanding of these institutions.

2002 marked a change in my work when I created the "Game of World Religious Art" that mapped the relations between art forms and different religions in a playful, consumer product. However it had not yet engaged with a key influence of Modern art, namely scatology, the study of filth.

It was scatology that led to abstract and figurative, mystical and moral, all being rejected in Gnosticism. Any meaning became an invalid. My art would catch up with this and also go beyond it. As I would expose how postmodernists had used scatology to reject all answers and yet they remained with consumerism and with Modernistic, atheistic, materialistic and anti-religious assumptions.

MODERN ART CONCLUSION

In human psychology and belief there is a need to balance moral systems (with their Gods) with a mystical Holism. We have seen how art can directly express these perspectives (figurative moral and abstract mystical) or indirectly express them as a way to achieve the psychological balance. I propose that this is an unconscious mechanism. However, art also has the conscious functions of expression, analysis and symbolism.

Most religious art was expressive or symbolic but Modern art is more analytic, part of a Modernist investigation into nature (the nature of art in this instance) which was begun by the Greeks. Art took on its own dynamic as an examination of nature and the nature of art.

Western society had become dominated by a belief in a moral God and art was figurative only as a re-examination of classical thinkers and mythology. A balance with the moral Gods of the West came with mystical Romanticism. Primitivism broung an Animistic viewpoint that paved the way for the Cubists and Futurists to violently break convention and focus on the dynamic machine age. The Abstract artists sought balance by expressing mystical ideals but other artists, like Chagall, sought a more pastoral focus on symbolically representing individuals as State abstraction grew in power.

Faced with the mania and destruction that technology had been used for by an unbalanced Western humanity there was a move to balance in figurative art that expressed human ideals. Chagall's personal expression was ignored by politicians in favour of Social Realism. This was used by Fascist and Communist countries to promote leaders like Hitler and Stalin and these figures took on quasi-religious and mystical status.

Meanwhile Dadists wanted to breakdown power structures and after the Second World War the Abstract Expressionists balanced against these figures and the mass produced figurative imagery that society had become saturated with. American Protestant society balanced its moral Christianity and its figurative consumerism with these Abstract Expressionists. These artists became institutionalised in a media driven society that became a Spectacle of images used for social control. Performance Artists wanted to break down and break free of this Spectacle with Gnostic performance, to reach the mystical that the Abstract Expressionists had intimated at but had failed to reach. Failure by the performance artists to achieve this change would eventually lead to postmodernism.

POSTMODERN ART

DEFINITIONS OF POSTMODERN

It is notoriously hard to define postmodernism as it is non-essentialist and against single, simple definitions, which it sees as modernist and controlling. So our definition will arise as we look at the work of various artists and thinkers. The postmodern views with the most influence on art practice and theory arises from continental philosophy.

These meta-narratives were questioned and broken down by the postmodernists. What united them was a rejection of grand schemes of political transformation and also a feeling of being trapped in a commodity system. The postmodernists sought to listen to the voices of marginalised and oppressed groups and to rebel against power structures. However, many of the thinkers were still trapped in Modernist, mystical perspectives that rejected religious beliefs, which was another grand narrative.

In "The Postmodern Condition" Jean-Francois Lyotard argued that what is regarded as scientific objectivity changes depending on social and cultural conditions. Knowledge is limited by the institutions and the rules they operate within. The truths and universal values that bind a society or ideology together and which claim to be objective in criticising other forms of knowledge are really just questionable meta-narratives (narratives about narratives)(66).

POSTMODERN CONSUMERISM

In response to feelings of being trapped within a commodity system, Andy Warhol was one of a number of artists who acknowledged, and worked with, their complicity with this system. In the 1960's Warhol, took mechanical means of reproduction and applied them to imagery from popular culture and advertising in work that was flat and with brash colours.

Warhol replaced Rothko's search for deep meaning with a search for money. Amongst his most famous images Warhol printed rows of red and white Campbell's Soup cans and printed "Marilyn", a giant head of Marilyn Monroe, with lurid yellow hair, bright pink face, and smeared red lips and teeth. These works show a belief that consumerism had become the most important force in American society.

Warhol began the worship of new, human Gods and icons of consumerism, like Marilyn Monroe. And those now in control of art were the buyers, the men of money and power, the men who now acted like they were the new Gods.

Warhol's portrait of 'Mao' 1974, a giant print of the head of the Chairman of the Chinese Communist party, showed how even communist imagery could be turned into a capitalist commodity, into pop icons. In his survey, of the American avant-garde since 1970, Henry. M. Sayre, Associate Professor of art at Oregon University states how Andy Warhol's "Maos" 1974 and "Hammer and Sickles" 1976 gave an empty reminder of how the political nature of art could be turned into commodity.

Warhol thought that even the avant-garde had become a marketable notion so artists must accept their market status to attempt to overcome it (67). He Andy Warhol accepted that life had become an empty, immanent commodity and reflected this in his figurative art work (A2 in our earlier schema).

Avant-garde artists once created shocking art to waken the bourgeoisie out of political complacency, but now Warhol used shock to thrill the bourgeoisie and make money. His paintings turned everything, even death (electric chairs, car crashes and skulls), into a commodity. In his paper for the 1985 Institute of Contemporary Arts conference on postmodernism Michael Newman questions how far Warhol was overcoming pop culture through deconstructing it, as even the deconstruction (that Taylor sees as true postmodernism) can be seen as complicit, careerist opportunism on the part of the artist (68).

The artist was now just a businessman with a factory where people made his artwork for him. This wasn't like the renaissance workshop of Michelangelo, it was a production line, churning out art.

Despite this, Warhol's religious works from the 1980s is the largest body of religious works by any major contemporary American artist. Warhol was openly homosexual but was secret about his Christian faith. It would have been bad for business. Even now galleries don't show works like his 1986 pictures of "Christ's Last Supper". They like his pictures of electric chairs and car crashes, not his pictures of Christ mixed with adverts for Potato Chips, Dove Soap, and General Electric. Maybe because it wasn't anti-Christian enough.

For a long time Rothko's abstract canvases were seen as more serious than Warhol's art. Maybe it was because New York art collectors came from a tradition of Protestant and Jewish simplicity, a tradition that rejected kitsch imagery. But eventually the collectors changed their focus because money now drove society more than religion and Warhol's art made icons of money and consumer goods.

Claudia Schmuckli, curatorial assistant at the Guggenheim says: "Advertising logos for Wise Potato Chips, Dove Soap, and General Electric (a feature of Warhol's pictures that can be traced back to his Campbell's soup cans of the early 1960s) superimposed on the figures of Christ and the Apostles, creating a hybrid of the sacred and profane, high art and commercial design. The seemingly heretical irreverence for these distinctions reflects the inevitable transformation of a deeply religious work into a cliché whose spiritual message has become muted through repetition."(69).

Warhol regularly went to church in New York and his art celebrates forms of consumer kitsch, however, it still suggests that Warhol had a need to use art as a pseudo-religious sacrament that can create some kind of personal change, breaking out of the media Spectacle through divine intervention or transubstantiation. And this is what makes the work postmodern.

However, the impossibility of this breaking out is theorised by Jean Baudrillard (70) who argued that when we approach places/objects/people our minds are already full of preconceptions given to us by media images of those places/objects/people. Brand names, cinematic stereotypes, music videos etc, are complete fantasy and when an object is mass produced, then a simulation of an original object becomes the real object.

Baudrillard argues that our image of reality begins as a reflection of reality, then becomes a mask of reality, then marks an absence of reality, then bear no relation to reality at all,. They become pure simulacrum (71). Signs no longer have a meaning as nothing is true and false. There is no sense of absolute reality and there is instead, "a proliferation of myths of origin and signs of reality:"

This system of simulations has become so widespread that there is no reality outside of this system and the simulations have taken on more importance than actual reality. As such they are a "hyperreality". All of our experiences are simulated and it is impossible to see the difference between natural and manufactured desires.

Baudrillard did not think that this was a deliberate process to keep people oppressed but rather he thinks that a society requires signs, codes and simulations to function. To escape simulation people may try to follow something that makes them feel that they are connecting back to something real but he thought that nothing can actually take people out of media simulations. Newman concludes that for Baudrillard simulation is the melancholy at the total sameness of everything as nothing can be seen as original, nor as copy.

I suggest that for Warhol even religion is simulation as he took images of images of religion and mixed them in commodified pictures of reality.

POSTMODERN BREAKDOWN

In opposition to Warhol's consumer postmodernism is a more radical, completely divided stance (72). This fits with Jean-Francois Lyotard's psychological model based around a divided self. Lyotard argues that the self is made of irreconcilable parts and that society (or culture) is similarly made of aspects that cannot be united (73). Thus the postmodern person is seen as having no fixed identity but rather as having multiple selves.

Poststructuralists, such as Jacques Derrida, also rejected any underlying, formal, single meanings because these were seen as totalitarian and imperialistic. Structuralists, such as the anthropologist Claude Levi-Strauss and the psychoanalyst Jacques Lacan, thought that systems of meaning were relatively fixed and complete but, in contrast, poststructuralists see them as fundamentally contradictory, open and unfinished (74).

Warhol's plastic glamorization of the female form had left women in a social role of sex object. But now artists began to question prescribed social identities and roles and to break them down.

Cindy Sherman is an American photographer who questioned the representation of women in society and the media. She photographed herself in a range of costumes in her "Complete Untitled Film Stills" (1977–1980). The photographs are black and white and are of Sherman as the actresses in shots from Hollywood pictures, B-movies, and film noir. She played with identity art, showing that we are divided, with many, different superficial media selves, none of which are our real identity.

In her photo-series, the 1981 "Centerfolds," she also points out that stereotyping of women in film, television and magazines. Sherman wanted a man to look at her with an expectation of something lascivious and then feel like a violator. However, the person who highlighted this concern about the male gaze was Annie Sprinkle, an American former prostitute, pornographic actress, sex film producer and performance artist.

In her "Public Cervix Announcement" performance she had spread legs and invited the audience to view her cervix with a speculum and flashlight. The cervix looks back at the male viewer, breaking down the masculine/ subject–object relationship where the male viewer dominates the female object with their gaze, rather than works together in feminine unity.

In 1991, Sprinkle later created the "Sluts and Goddesses" workshop where she played with religious identities. As have many musician artists from the 1980's onwards. Popular musicians such as David Bowie played with identities and roles such as Ziggy Stardust and then Nina Hagen took on religious identities such as the Virgin Mary or as the Hindu Goddess Kali. Sprinkle took this further, performing

"The Legend of the Ancient Sacred Prostitute", in which she did a "sex magic" masturbation ritual on stage. However, these artists were more sincere and less ironic in their adoption of these identities than Sherman and this return to ideas of magic, mysticism and art developed out of a return to a Gnostic breakdown of structures.

A writer who theorized the breakdown of male thought structures further was Jacques Derrida. Ward says that Derrida, in his deconstructive work, sees words as having multiple meanings. And "Deconstruction" is a process used to also show the hidden assumptions of different fields of knowledge. Derrida deconstructs these by saying communication is a text and is subject to "differance" where the meaning of a word cannot be fixed and does not stand by itself but is part of a context of other words. Thus no term has a fixed essence as it is defined in relation to what it is not, and is a differance. Texts strive to achieve a coherence but this is illusory and there is no fixed meaning to be found (75).

Derrida also considered that we naturally think by way of opposites, such as public/private, body/soul, subject/object. And that one term defines itself by way of rejecting the other term but it can often be found to have properties of the term that it rejects (76). So by analysing the relationship between the opposites in a text then the power structure can be investigated. Thus identities and meanings are not fixed but are often imposed through non-essential power relations.

Derrida also creates a space for this freedom of identity with the idea of the Chora (first proposed by Plato in the "Timaeus"). This is an empty space and a realm of possibility, in opposition to an actual revealing (77). Derrida says that "Plato figures chora as feminine – "the mother, the matrix, or the nurse." And yet, these "names" are improper, for chora is neither masculine not feminine but a third gender that approximates the neuter."" But here is where his own position is deconstructed, away from a third gender and into a bias towards the feminine (78). By making his philosophy more radical this is the beginning of a move away from difference and towards a Gnostic, mystical unity.

Art theorists have favoured this Chora. In "Revolution in Poetic Language" Julia Kristeva sees the Chora as a place of open possibility, a feminine and maternal source that the created world comes from (79). Ward describes how in "Revolution in Poetic Language" Julia Kristeva argues that women have been pushed to the boundaries in literature and art. Masculine texts have features such as structure, intelligibility and stability so texts with diverse and unstable meanings can help to undermine male discourse. Male society rejects unfixed and multiple identities but varied use of language can increase the range of possible identities imaginable and free you from an imagined unity of the self. Progressive works of art for Kristeva are "fragmentary, incomplete, non-systematic and ultimately inexplicable." (80)

This is a similar line of thought (about a breakdown to formlessness) that Georges Bataille took to an extreme and that collapsed into a transcendent unity. Taylor explains how, in "Theory of Religion", Bataille developed a rethinking of Friedrich Nietzsche's notions of the Apollonian and the Dionysian"(81). Apollo is the ancient Greek god of the sun, music, poetry, morality, self-control and freedom from self control. Dionysus is the ancient Greek god of wine, mystical ecstasy and intoxication. Neither can exist without the other. In Apollo we can achieve an illusion of rationality but in Dionysus lays the return to the maternal womb of being, a realm that people long to return to and where the individual self disappears (82). This being is the primordial oneness of Derrida's Chora (83) and it is here that extreme division leads to a Modernist, utopian unity.

Here the personality is disintegrated in a Dionysian style ritual. Difference is transformed into the unity of the Chora by transgressive acts, that violate the boundaries between violence and eroticism, that break down the separation between different possible modes of being. Like Bakhtin, he believed that festivals are the place where this energy is most manifest. And he saw that sacrifice breaks the profane order and that the greatest sacrifice is the self and selfhood, completed with death (84).

This breakdown is a form of Gnostic Drama, like that of Anton Artaud, who aimed to create radical difference in his theatre in order to transcend rationality. In Artaud's Gnostic drama cruelty meets cruelty in a sublime horror that is not just against language but against the body, the created world (85) and against the notion of a creator God/demi-urge (86). "Artaud equates creation with cruelty and proposes to undertake the work of counter-cruelty in his theatre" (87). Artaud proposes a form of self-(re)creation where the human returns to Sophia, the "mother" of the demiurge.

This art is a development of modernist formless Gnosticism and a theoretical framework for art work that relates to the Chora can be seen in "Liminal Acts A Critical Overview of Contemporary Performance and Theory" by Susan Broadhurst.

"liminal performance similarly presents a deconstruction of binary opposition, which is demonstrated in the collapse of hierarchical distinctions such as those between high and mass/popular culture. Central to the liminal is a mixing of popular knowledge with "elitist" knowledge, together with a definite blurring of set boundaries; in other worlds a certain intertextuality is presented. Other aesthetic features that are present in the liminal and parallel Nietzsche's "active interpretation" are playfulness and the celebration of the surface "depthlessness of culture", together with a stylistic bricolage and the mixing of codes. (88)

Broadhurst believes liminal creations can have a cultural effect by creating new visions of possibility outside of what is expected in society. And we can see this in the work of the New York artists Robert Mapplethorpe and Ron Athey whose sado-masochistic photographs reconstructed sexualised versions of religious devotion in the lives of martyrs and Saints.

Robert Mapplethorpe took glossy black and white photographs of scenes of semi-religious devotion and sexual violence. But the devotion was to explicit, hardcore homosexual acts. A fist being shoved up a man's anus, a man in sadomasochists' leather clothing urinating in another man's mouth, a finger being pushed into the tip of an erect penis and a naked man hung upside down on an inverted crucifix.

In "Self Portrait" 1978, Mapplethorpe had taken a photograph of himself from behind. He was dressed in a waistcoat and seat-less leather pants. His hair was in a wild abandon, as if allowing the unfettered flow of his desires, and sporting a goatee beard. He looked defiantly over his shoulder, at the viewer, as he inserted the handle of a bull whip, as if it was the Devil's tail, into his anus.

"Self Portrait" 1985 is a close up of Mapplethorpe's face. Eyes, surrounded with eye liner, looked out, piercingly, behind dark hair that descended to the sensuous curve of his naked shoulders. But protruding from this hair were pointy ears and horns in the manner of Satan, Lucifer, the most beautiful, outcast angel. The Angel who rebelled against the Demi-urge.

For Mapplethorpe the perfect, gay body was a manifestation of the divine. Here he is Dionysus, the God of intoxication and nature, who the Christians called the Devil because they did not understand him. Dionysus had two horns, one of life and creation, the other of death and destruction. Pleasure, pain and fear were the materials of Mapplethorpe's art and he photographed acts of sexual punishment and martyrdom because bitter sweet sex was sacred to him. His aim was an ecstatic transformation away from the chains of the "civilised" world. Tragically, 4 years after this portrait, he died from A.I.D.S.

An inheritor of his tradition, of rejection of institutions in a Gnostic symbolism, is the performance artist Ron Athey. In Athey's 2002, performance, the "Solar Anus." The naked, bald, heavily tattooed artist spread the cheeks of his backside to show a black flaming sun tattooed around his anus. This was a black hole of darkness and he was pulling a string of pearls from out of it. He sat upon a throne, lifting a golden jester's crown, with hooks fixed to both it and his face. The hooks pulled his bleeding skin upwards as he crowned himself Sun King mocking the God Apollo. Then he powdered his face and was sodomising himself, with dildos attached to his shoes.

In his "Solar Anus" performances the pierced, A.I.D.S. infected Athey is in pain. But the more pain, blood and horror that he creates, the more value he finds. The name, "Solar Anus," comes from an essay by George Bataille, who used erotic deviance and human sacrifice to overthrow the rationalism, science and materialism of Modernity. Bataille wanted to escape the world and to reach a sacred black star, the Solar Anus. In this ecstasy is the union of Death (Thanatos) and Love (Eros). Athey is overcoming his corruptible flesh, in the eternal ecstasy of Thanateros. His souls in ecstasy.

Franco B is another performer and his "I Miss You!" performance is like a catwalk fashion show, but his hairless body is naked, painted white and then he cuts himself and lets himself bleed onto a canvas as he walks up and down. This is to confront the human form at its most existential and essential. He then makes art objects from the canvas that is bled upon.

Whilst this self-mutilation can be sacrificial and an investigation into primal religion it is more about investigating that older mode of being than actually returning to it. It can resemble an Animistic ritual with symbolic content or a more thorough Gnostic shock on the senses. The sacrifice also need not involve immediate physical pain or endurance, it can also be the pain from the artist exposing themselves emotionally.

In Marina Abramovic's "The House With the Ocean View" 2002 the artist is transformed by the performance where she created her living space in the gallery and created a space of no time, of the here and the now. It was three separate white boxes, one with a bed, one with a living space and one with a toilet and shower. The spaces were separated by ladders down to the gallery floor. All her functions were watched. People would visit for an occasional minute or regularly for hours. Marina says that she felt love towards the people that came to view her and look her in the eye. It was an un-materialistic piece of work where she aimed to expose her emotional and private self, creating discomfort in herself and the viewer. However, the more extreme the work the less likely it would be appropriated or copied by mainstream culture, e.g. Abramovic's work now resembles reality TV shows like Big Brother.

Some artists have also created performance work with a clear mystical intention, e.g. Zhang Huan's "Peace 1" 2001 where the artist was painted gold and suspended horizontally with the top of his head facing a giant temple bell inscribed with Chinese characters.

He is replacing the wooden beam that strikes the bell. Much of Huan's work is about feats of endurance, this he says is to explore his body to find out where he is from and who he is. He tries to do the impossible, e.g. to melt a bed of ice with his body, so that he can get to understand that he cannot change life and that things are predestined. He sees Buddhism as a way for people to make life better for themselves, to calm themselves down, to help other people and to forget themselves (89).

Another performance artist who has pushed his body to the limits of physical endurance (since the 1970's) is Genesis P-Orridge, who inherited the tradition of Aleistair Crowley, an occultist of the early twentieth century who explored various forms of Magick and Theosophy.

P-Orridge had a large following with his Temple of Psychic Youth. In "As It Is" Julie Wilson states that: "TOPY (Thee Temple ov Psychic Youth) was an exquisite piece of paratheatre, although this is not to say that it did not possess within and interlaced through its somewhat clichéd orthodoxies and practice models associated with most forms of organised religion, some valuable insights, cynical reflections on the gullibility and insecurities of human beings, and lessons in sexual freedom." (92)

In his TOPY, with its combination of music and religious style observance, he was seen as a mysterious messiah-style public figure. However, the magical practices involved mystical Gnosis and transformation and did not rely upon on the worship of a moral Divine being. Although his work is more like Animism, which has a more popular appeal than the esoteric Gnosticism.

Paul Cecil, in Even Further: The Metaphysics of Sigils, describes P-Orridges work as owing much to deconstruction in a use of montage that attacks social norms but also as going beyond "making us think", and is a literal attempt to "affect the real" through Magick. Thus the artwork becomes an actual tool to create change (90). His work is all about continuous change, to destabilise and activate energy to bring about more change. This energy can also be channelled into specific goals through the use of sigils (symbols constructed from a word, or phrase, or images of desired effects) that are given power through ritual and sexual practice.

P-Orridge let out wails, screams and unearthly noises as his band broke down any sense of melody and as images of destruction were projected onto a large screen behind him at Preston Guildhall in 2000. He was deconstructing our view and as the breakdown continued a rotating abstract shape was projected, a new sigil reminiscent of the Psychic TV logo that he used in the 80's and the word "Process" was flashed upon the screen.

P-Orridge has constantly experimented with changing identities and gender roles. Hence his name, Genesis P-Orridge – an undefined, primal matter, like the primal soup in the Chora. His early work included living with the performance group COUM in a house where everyday the performers took new clothing and identities out of a box and they had to live these personas.

P-Orridge's work also involved explorations of the limits of his own body's sense of pleasure and pain. In his 2002 exhibition in A22 Gallery, London, there were photographs of his transition to resemble the gender of his partner, Lady Jackie, by having breast implants (and her having breast reductions) in a creative being called Breyer P-Orridge. This hermaphrodite status was viewed by P-Orridge, in an article for "Independent on Sunday", as an alchemical, evolutionary progression - linking to the mystical union of opposites (91).

As with so many performance artists, this surgery has links to the bodily mortification of Christ on the cross. P-Orridge also showed a large, image of the head of Christ (taken from a Catholic prayer card) and had imposed beneath it a photograph of his new chest with breast implants in a Modernist, mystical union of opposites. His focus is on the continual recreation of identity and never on the fixing of an identity. He emphasises process and the liminal unreality of identity.

A further example of a mystical ritual performer is the artist Alex Grey, whose "Chapel of Sacred Mirrors" 1979-2004 is a gallery that shows some of his characteristic works. These painted canvases and mirrors showing anatomical images of the energy flows around people in states of meditation and mystical Enlightenment. The veins and body parts are quite shocking and show the bodily nature of existence but the lights and aura's around these bodies show how existence is transcended. Grey is less concerned with breakdown of structures and is more literal in his representing abstract, mystical states on the physical body whilst also incorporating some traditional religious imagery (in our schema A1, A2 and B1). Like many of these artists he has heavy influences from both mysticism and L.S.D. psychedelic experiences.

The above artists mark the continued attempt to find redemption through self-sacrifice or shock and foreboding in a piece of artwork. The artists becomes like the incarnate God who is sacrificed to save the believers (the audience.). However, the utopia sought is a mystical consciousness with a focus on Dionysus. The true salvation is for the select few artists and the sacrifice is for the small band of art followers. There is no political change other than gender and sexual politics are given a voice and shock art tactics to raise awareness. Nothing is done with this awareness and it remains largely confined to the gallery system.

An example of how this mysticism has even become embraced in the gallery system is in the Surreal symbolism of Matthew Barney (an artist who was perhaps the American answer to the Young British Artists who we shall look at next). He proposes a mystical resolution, theorised in his work, yet the slick, superficial, commodity veneer of his work is also devoid of mystical transcendence.

Barney's "Cremaster Cycle" 1995 - 2002 is a sumptuous cinematographic film that uses symbolic, surreal imagery in a liminal balancing of opposites. Imagery of sport, sacrifice, execution, glamour, motor-vehicles, New York's Chrysler building, Freemasons, animal-human hybrids and semi-naked bodies combine in a semi-narrative that has no definite conclusion so as to remain in a state of liminality and eternal recurrence. The symbol used throughout the series of five films is a vertical phallus through a horizontal line of the feminine. The institutionalisation of esoteric Gnosticism is clear as in the main conclusion he charts the progression of the main protagonist through the various stages of Freemasonry whilst climbing the levels of the Guggenheim art museum in New York.

More contemporary examples of a Gnostic position can also involve digital technology. Miao Xiaochun is a visual artist who has recreated Michelangelo's "The Last Judgment in Cyberspace" 2006 using 3D digital modelling software to create a digital avatar of his own body. He then modelled this onto all of the 400-plus figures from Michelangelo's famous "The Last Judgment" Sistine Chapel painting. All the characters, divine, demonic, saved or damned are the same figure. All distinctions are dissolved. The figures form a 3D environment that can be viewed from different angles and the images have a sublime and apocalyptic immediacy. However, the eyes of the figures have no pupils and so have a haunting and demonic quality that rejects the created world.

The artist Sumit Sarkar also used digital graphics to create a series of sculptures and projections on the themes of Hindu Gods in an abstracted iconography. The project was called "The Ananta Experience" 2009. These images are dark and foreboding, taking you to a feeling of the destructive power of the Hindu Goddess Kali, an icon of deconstruction.

I argue that this radical division of deconstruction concludes in a spiritual Gnosticism that, like Schelling's philosophy, is still a part of a Modernist mysticism. Artistically it fits with B1 in our schema. This mysticism is a form of Utopian unity and if Modernism is associated with unity and utopia whereas postmodernism is associated with division. However, I propose that postmodern division is non-extreme, non-radical and non-destructive. That a postmodern position allows people to live indecisively with or without semi-ironic faith in a resolution in utopian unity. And that artistically it should fit with A2 in our schema.

THE END OF MODERNIST UTOPIAN POLITICAL UNITY

The end of a Modernist Utopia has been a theme for postmodern artists. Interviewed for the catalogue of the 50th Venice Art Biennale (2003) Immanueal Wallerstein (1) stated that the term Utopia was invented by Sir Thomas More in the 16th century. It means "nowhere" in Greek as a Utopia is seen as an imagining of an ideal society. An artist who rejects that modernist utopian thinking, can bring complete change but celebrates the energy it has against consumer society, is Thomas Hirschhorn.

Okuwi Enwezor suggested, in "The Black Box", his introduction to the exhibition catalogue for "Documenta XI" (2002), that Ground Zero is a site that appears to define politics and art for the 21st century. He suggests that it is both a destruction of an old perspective and a tabula rasa where a new perspective can be built (93). Consequently Hirschhorn's womb-like "Cavemanman" 2002, his first major show in New York, could represent the birth (or defecation) of the viewer back out of a tabula rasa into the world of consumerism – with nothing left but an energy for change.

"Cavemanman" was a cave made of wrapping tape and cardboard. As I entered the white cube gallery I was placed in an environment where nothing was left uncovered. I moved around the space, walking up ramps, along levels and into subsidiary grottoes and cul-de-sacs. I had to negotiate around boulders and rocks made out of cardboard boxes covered in masking tape.

The central grotto of the cave system was a "living" space where a "tribe" of shop dummy type figures was covered with gold tin-foil. They were linked by umbilical like, foil tentacles to academic books such as John Rawls' "Theory of Justice" and to fake bombs. This represented a world of idealistic thinking and suggested that idealistic political change occurs only by violent means.

The utopian idealism was also represented as doomed to failure as cans of coke and sprite littered the floor in an excess of cultural waste.

The tin-foil family represents us all as being consumers in a failed idealism. This womb-like Chora does not offer the possibility of Gnostic mysticism, just rebirth into the material world of the Demi-urge. As when we leave the gallery we are symbolically re-born, from the womb-like cave, back into the world as brand new consumers.

In an essay in the "Village Voice", entitled "More Is More", (94) Kim Levin likens the cave to an intestinal tract and I think that this reinforces Hirschhorn's interest in using trash and "low" materials– as intensines process food into waste. Levins feels that the dramatic juxtaposition of idealism and physical trash reinforces Hirschhorn's presentation of the failure of Utopianism – represented as ancient history unfulfilled in empty consumerism.

Hirschhorn uses art theory that is anti-consumerism and, to coincide with his Bataille Monument at Documenta XI, he commissioned Christopher Fiat to write an essay on Bataille, called "The Experience of Violence in Sacrifice" (99). This described Batailles' rejection of ideas of commodification and related to the semi-sacrificial/altar spaces that Hirschhorn creates to suggest an energy that cannot be commodified.

Hirschhorn joins both elite/academic theory and popular kitsch by transforming them both into trash. Hirschhorn puts general theoretical objects (e.g. books and pages) and popular objects (e.g. baseball caps and Rolex watches) inside low materials (e.g. masking tape and cardboard). The theories and objects are transformed into garbage to show their consumer nature as commodities. By using trash Hirschhorn critiques consumerism and challenges the elitism of the art object. But for Hirschhorn dialectical theory has reached an impasse and only the uncritical energy (and not the ideas) of the theorist offers hope.

Hirschhorn described his "fan" monument to Georges Bataille (Bataille Monument, Documenta XI, Kassel 2002) at the "Reports from the Fields of Visual Culture" conference at the Victoria Miro Gallery, London 2003. By putting the monument in a housing complex and not a historic site Hirschhorn critiqued the notion of a monument (and its location) as something that is fixed and grandiose. Bataille had nothing to do with Kassell and his monument could be shown anywhere. The monument had many different facets including a social complex of buildings, with library and exhibition.

The library in the monument had books on subjects like art, sport and sex, but nothing on Bataille. This was in order to emphasise Bataille as a celebrity rather than his political writings and the exhibition gave information about the life of Bataille rather than his works. There was a snack bar that served as a focal point for the local community and a TV studio for local residents to make programmes about their day at the monument.

Hirschhorn saw himself as an equal co-worker. Residents were asked to help and were given pay and when the monument was dismantled the parts were taken away by them. This was like the social art of Beuys - but I don't think that any critical direction remained from the project.

Other artists who use packaging materials and rubbish to look at social ideals are Michael Landy and Tomoto Takahashi.

In "High Art Lite" Julian Stallabrass says that Landy invented his own fictional corporate identity, "Scrapheap Services" with the aim of clearing away surplus people from society. In "Scrapheap Services" (1995) "dummies dressed in corporate cleaning uniforms sweep up thousands of tiny human figures cut out from drink cans, McDonald's packaging and other detrituis" (95). The tiny figures are stamped with corporate colours and logos.

Landy took this further in his "Breakdown" 2001, which took place in an empty department store in London. This was converted into a factory for the systematic destruction of all of Landy's possessions. Each possession was itemised, put on a conveyor belt and then shredded. This act of rejection seems to be an attempt to escape from the effects of commodification but Landy then transformed his work in a series of etchings of common weeds called "Nourishment". The weeds were collected from urban sites and were a laborious study that referred more to botanical works than to romantic high art. (96) It suggested a guarded optimism that out of a complete rejection of consumerism it seems that "real" natural life can arise. This is not a mystical Gnosticism.

Stallabrass also describes how Tomoko Takahashi creates complex three dimensional installations and collages out of waste materials. "Beaconsfield" 1997 was an installation where trash was laid on the floor of a darkened gallery space and separated into sections by white lines. The trash was lit by an assortment of lamps and standing lights. Machines in the installation, e.g. a slide projector and tape recorder, continually played and on an old telephone face was written the word "process" (97). The work suggested that everything is subject to consumer ordering, including art, and that nothing has more value than anything else.

In redisplaying "Beaconsfield" for the Saatchi show "New Neurotic Realism" in 1999 Takahashi made clear her ideas about the "process" of constructing the work, - seemingly halted at an arbitrary point, to show the continual process of creation (98). Stallabras thinks that by showing the construction, cost, labour and issues of ownership criticism of the commodification of art were made. Here no resolution was offered and the work remained within the gallery system. However, coupled with this focus on trash is a focus on low, primitive elements of society, linking to the Primitivism of Gauguin.

An artistic attempt to critique the society of the Spectacle can be seen in urban pastoral art. Stallabras suggests that the pastoral is the view that simple living often produces values and truths which more sophisticated people have lost site of. (100) I think that Tracy Emin's "My Bed" 1999 is a good example of this. It is a reconstruction of her untidy bed (with litter and used menstrual stained underwear) that she had stayed in for several days in a period of suicidal depression over her relationship problems. The depictions of her life express to us some truth that she was not fully aware of and helps us to be aware of in our own lives.

Another example is Sarah Lucas, whose "Two Fried Eggs and a Kebab" 1992 is two fried eggs and a kebab on a table that is a surreal symbol of a woman. This was built on with her photographic "Self Portrait With Fried Eggs" 1996 where she sits in an armchair in jeans and t-shirt with two fried eggs covering her breasts.

Stallabras, however, criticises this kind of work as being fashionable but with no real political comment. (101) Roberts in "Domestic Squabble" is more sympathetic. He suggests that the localism and micro-narratives of this kind of work are in opposition to Globalism and the promise of grand narratives with their "Hegelian big sweeps of periods and epochs." (102) He concludes that they showed the gap that existed between the lives of ordinary people and the promises of critical theory, however, he warns that in doing this they have also rejected the vocabulary for making critical statements (103).

Stallabras thinks that that Beech and Roberts' "Philistine debate" supports urban pastoral artwork but that such artwork does not force a clear cultural definition or closure. It creates a liminality that serves no critical purpose (104). The work critiques Modernity and presents a breakdown but offers no real alternative.

In contrast to this Malcolm Quinn in "The Legions of the Blind: the Philistine and Cultural Studies" suggests a critical use of the notion of the Philistine. He thinks that "culture" is seen the primary source of alienation in humanity because it contains within it (105) the idea of the Philistine and so implies the idea of alienation and that this alienation forms part of critical, Marxist thinking. Thus work that explores Philistine perspectives keep open the possibility of there being critical thinking.

In his introduction to "Documenta XI" Okuwi Enwezor called for a more inclusive and global art that addressed the marginalized ethnic groups and was process based, rather than making conclusive statements (106). He viewed Ground Zero as a Tabula Rasa that characterised de-colonisation and introduced cultures on the periphery into the centre. He also called for a dialogue between Westernism and Islam. (107)

I think that the notion of the Philistine is integral as whilst Enwezor called for the inclusion of marginal groups and as the origin of the word Palestine is from Philistine (108) I think that the Islamic faith in Palestine, and of other religious faiths, presents the last major "Philistinism" to challenge Western consumer culture.

And in New York there were artists who used religion to fight against the conmmodity system. The Revd Billy (Bill Talen) used consumer icons in a bricolage involving a Christian preaching style and anti-consumer performances. He deconstructed advertising and consumerism to give moral messages about unfair trade and how profits are mis-used by multinational corporations.

He questioned and interrupted patterns of consumption by performing in public spaces and inside corporate chain stores, where the shopping experience was most ritualized. His activities including entering Starbucks cafes (preaching about the political and social effects of consumerism and the record of Starbucks for corporate ruthlessness) and entering Disney stores (throwing around Mickey Mouse dolls, proclaiming Mickey to be the anti-Christ) have often led to his arrest.

His performance role-play as an evangelical preacher, with his gospel choir, was only mocking in the first instance: "We shout "Hallelujah!" together, and it's funny for a moment, but then you're on a journey after that, toward trying to solve something about a local community garden or trying to protect a person who's had an independent business on the corner for thirty years, and they're getting run out of town by NASDAQ funny-money from some chain store. And when we pray, it becomes prayer. Do I want to use the word "prayer"? No. But we address the god/goddess/mystery thing. That's the latest thing we call it, the god/goddess/mystery thing. And you don't do that from a position of parody. So "Reverend Billy" is just a way to meet and greet. The parody's over in seconds (135).

This suggests that a genuine religious or mystical sentiment can arise out of a semi-ironic statement. The Reverend Billy's rejection of commodity also includes a rejection of religion itself, but this still allows a genuine sentiment to appear: "We have a sort of post-religion spirituality," he says. "But we never use the word religion, we never use the word spirituality. All those words we consider to be products in themselves. They are all bankrupt. They are all used by people we don't want to emulate."(136).

Revd Billy is avant-garde as he actively tries to stand outside of the consumer system and opposes it. He believes that the Iraq war was caused by consumerism and that the effects of the war are hidden from the American public. An example of a service is one held at St. Mark's Church, New York City, Tax Day 2002. After the worship the church of stop shopping preached on the steps of a New York Post Office; talking to people posting their tax returns whilst the Stop Bombing Gospel Choir sang. And whilst this opposition is outwardly religious it still has a Modernist Utopian basis (not a mystical Gnostic basis), something that many artist still assume as part of their cultural norm.

The work of these artists is a mixture of A1, A2 B1 and B2. It is like the Dadaists, who broke down standard imagery to give an undefined moral, political message (B2) or a mystical, Gnostic breakdown (A1). Any positive moral statement was given symbolically (A2) as was any mystical message (B2).

BREAKDOWN AND ANTI-RELIGIOUS RECONSTRUCTION IN YOUNG BRITISH ARTISTS

A group of artists that developed a different approach to this failed utopia and the inescapability of consumer culture were the Young British Artists. This group included Tracy Emin, Damien Hirst and the Chapman brothers. They had a complex relation of celebrity, politics, atheism and punk rock. Just like punk rock, Brit Art had an association with the glamorisation of social disorder, crime and violence, and both have become a part of the British establishment. Punk and Brit Art arose in a Thatcherist Conservative capitalist atmosphere associated with individual freedom as being seen as more important than social concern. And the advertising Guru and collector of the art of the YBAs, Charles Saatchi, contributed to this atmosphere in his advertising campaigns for the conservative party.

In "High Art Lite" Stallabras sees the YBA's as rejecting the deep psychology and metaphysics of traditional Modern art (109) and as seeing social responsibility and moral sense as no longer ideologically possible (110).

In their place the YBAs confront the viewer with the abject and destabilize fixed meaning. The work never makes closure and is not further justified or explained because the work has an anti-theoretical base and is autonomous from theory. Stallabras notes that the demise of the Avant-garde left no single, clear political stance and that the postmodern ideals fell into consumerism. (111)

The YBAs give us crude visual pleasures that cause liberalist moral objections (112) and conceptual one-liners that make an immediate impact (113).

On (114) Stallabras notes how American critic Alexandra Anderson-Spiby viewed "Sensation" as a lesser imitation of earlier work by international artists. Stallabras goes on to say (115) that American critics David Frankel and Robert Storr dislike the YBA art for being local, naïve and parodic. This original combination (of international style and provincial content), however, is seen as a strength by Roberts in "Domestic Squabbles".

Stallabras says that many YBAs glorify the urban as the pastoral once was glorified (116). The proletariat is seen as the "natural" worker but when the artist takes on the role of being this worker then they cannot give a theoretical meaning to their work without destroying this naturalist stance. Yet he thinks that they do have a stance of consumer selfishness. This conservatism is passed off as socialism as Stallabras says that the YBAs have an oceanic oneness with everything, that fits with Tony Blair's New Labour, with art joined to the working class in a classless class (117). Stallabras, however, notes how the art of the YBAs is patronizing to the working class by seeing them as dirty, violent and sex focussed.

John Roberts, in "Domestic Squabbles" (118) says that whilst the YBA work reduced the possibility of historical and critical debate for art but it also expanded the possibilities for art to go outside the academy and to include the everyday. However, in putting high culture and low culture in opposition Stallabras (119) says that extreme reactions from both camps were created, and not a liminal suspension of judgement as intended. The display of Marcus Harvey's "Myra" in the "Sensation" exhibition is used as an example of this, where the press went into 2 opposing camps at the painting of the child murderer Myra Hindley made out of childrens' handprints.

Stallabrass thinks there is also a contradiction as the YBA world is fragmented but so much is made of the artists personality (120) e.g. Tracey Emin as authentic, primitive and spiritual in her honesty and Damien Hirst as bad boy art celebrity.

Stallabras notes another contradiction. Whilst the YBAs reject moral statements they also seek admiration for their attempt to be brutally honest and Matthew Collings says "Their trick, which so far has been completely effective, is to make all this seem very tied to real problems of modern life" (121).

This suggests that there is no real attempt to overcome consumerism or moral systems in a Gnostic mysticism or Socialist political Utopia. Rather it is about the artist as a Godlike celebrity, which follows in the footsteps of Salvador Dali.

Since the late 1960's and early 1970's the Gnostic Modernists wanted shock people and to wake them up, to make them think and feel in a different way. So they promoted dark, artists who used their own bodies in performance art to unite violence and eroticism, death and life. They broke-down the artificial moralities of the modern state and its power structures into a "formless" equality. But this rebellion was not just against Modernism, it was against the original authoritarian figure. It was against God, the "author" of the universe.

Cruelty, horror and sexual desire were used to humiliate and disintegrate the personality, to shock humanity into waking up from rationality, so that they could see their mystical core. A Gnostic state where opposites, like the sacred and the secular, are united.

However, because the mystical liminality of these artists was too elitist to be followed it created a vacuum and the love of money, the lowest common denominator, filled that void. That is why artists now used shocking images. It was just advertising, to grab attention for their work so it could be sold for a higher price. It was brutal economic Darwinism, survival of the fittest. It was as if the artists had all made a pact with the Devil. All this art-world seemed to really cared about was money, sex and power.

At this time people still assumed art was just about personal taste and that the monetary value was dictated by personal taste not any objective system. The artists also hid behind the aura of exclusivity and esotericism that the art-world produced, and did not mind collectors or themselves not understanding the theories behind art. Art became about market forces.

Damien Hirst became famous for this, but he could not have done it without being promoted by the advertising mogul Charles Saatchi.

Hirst's work expresses the triumph of the free-market. He was promoted by the advertising mogul Charles Saatchi, the man that led the advertising for Margaret Thatcher's election campaign, promoting the free market "ethic," and the man that helped Nicholas Serota get appointed, by Margaret Thatcher, as the Director of the Tate Galleries.

Hirst and the YBAs inherited Salvador Dali's Surreal art and sense of artist as Divine. However, Hirst expressed this the most. He was the Messiah of art who commodified animal sacrifices and nightmarish images of bloodletting, even mocking the divine by giving his dissected cows in formaldehyde religious titles like "Mother and Child" (1994). And the celebration of it was like the Old Testament blasphemous celebration of the Golden Calf (Hirst even made a Golden Calf in formaldehyde to relate his work to this).

The work was not even that original. Stealing ideas is rife in commerce and art is commerce. It's just like supermarkets squeezing out corner shops and like corporations taking-over small companies. Only legal definitions change the common sense understanding of the term "stealing" in order to make it acceptable for the rich and powerful, e.g. Hirst's diamond skull "For the Love of God" 2007, (that used 8,601 diamonds and had real body parts in it) was reputedly plagiarised off artist John LeKay who had been producing similar jewel encrusted skulls and who had exhibited with Hirst in 1994. Hirst's "Valium" 2000 painting was claimed to be copied from Robert Dixon's drawing "True Daisy" 1984 only the geometrical spots were reversed.

Hirst's work glorified in bloodletting and eroticism but also in the superficial world of fashion. He commodified even the most severe of sacrificial Dionysian imagery in order to provide a quick thrill. However, nothing beyond is intimated or appealed to, there is no redemption and this atheistic consumerism contradicts the religious theme of his work. His nihilistic perspective is never in doubt. Such full irony and atheism is more Modernist than the semi-irony of postmodernism.

Julian Stallabras describes Hirst's nihilistic work as being an unredemptive personal complicity with the market. An investment in his work is a status symbol and will potentially reap economic rewards (appreciation in value). This enslaves artist and buyer within an economic system, rather than liberates them from it, offer any positive direction or even look at the tension between belief and unbelief.

Damien Hirst was the God or Messiah of this system and his "Romance in the Age of Uncertainty" exhibition, White Cube 2003, was a commodified, contemporary art presentation of Catholic style relics of saints. His 12 disciples were represented as severed cows heads in formaldehyde tanks. The idea of relics of saintly bodies also contrasted with Hirst's atheistic and pseudo-scientific presentation of these bodies in a Modernist investigation of the body under the medical surgeon's knife or as a butcher's commodity.

The carnal nature of Hirst's work reinforced the galleries ability to transform base materials into money and the work was brutal and aggressive. The domination and power of the corporate mediaeval church is mirrored in the domination of the corporate art world. The exhibition shows a brutal materialism that either reinforces faithlessness or makes you turn away and cling to the faith that you have.

The only Romanticism is in the Sublime power of the art commodity institution to threaten to engulf the individual. Even the notion of the artist as an individual is replaced by the artist as appropriator and corporate finance machine. The viewer is deconstructed and has to reconstitute themselves and their values. The sense of helplessness comes from the institutional display and its unstoppable marketing machine rather than the work itself.

Whatever liminality that he generates is soon replaced with atheistic consumerism that rejects anything other than his own status as the dominant artist. As such the work is not Modernist Gnostic mysticism, however, it is Modernist atheism and materialist consumerism. The work reinforces his own moral status so it fits with A2 in our schema but comes from a negative or evil moral position, i.e. an immoral position.

Other YBA artists who articulate a more nuanced religious direction are the Chapman brothers, Jake and Dinos. There work has more relation to Dadaism but it is still rooted in Dali's Surrealism.

The Zygotes in the Chapman's Eden called "Six Feet Under" are manikins of children that are cut up and reassembled, joined like Siamese twins, with multiple limbs wearing trainers and with protruding penises and anuses for noses and mouths. They are mutations of consumerism and show a naked sexuality twisting into unnatural forms. They represent a selfish, capitalist domination of nature and the breaking down of social structures but offer nothing to replace them.

In their interview with Douglas Foght, (122) the Chapmans say that their work is "dramatically anti conception. We always claim that it doesn't pertain to any kind of meaning. If anything, it pertains to an attack on conscious meaning, which we see conceptual art as constantly prioritizing". They go on to state that their work is non-political because it is scatological and tries to break down culture by rejecting language and structures of power. To do this they seek a libidinal discharge that is not representational but is iconic, directly relating to the unconscious.

In their interview with Maia Damianovic (123) the Chapmans say how they are breaking down the "self". They are against singularities, the notion of an autonomous self, humanism and the notion of God. They go on to say that want to create a kind of convulsion between oppositions that relates to the Kantian notion of the Sublime and produces a cultural value of nil.

Mark Sladen in Art Monthly (124) describes their work as a reaction to fragmentation and that they, like other contemporary artists, have used the body to have the appearance of being an "authentic" expression. Their re-unified bodies use fragments, fetishes or traces to reclaim the body from technological fragmentation. However, they also celebrate the breakdown of identity and think that entropy is an inevitable reaction to attempts to form identity.

In "Gender is an Organic Superstition" (125) the Chapmans also explain that they think that sexual difference arises from out of our sense of having a separate ego. So they sees to transgress that split of nature and technology via genetics. The hybrid forms are iconic of our inner selves and part of the shock is in seeing ourselves reflected.

In Doctorin' the Retardis (in Chapmanworld) David Falconer (126) says that "in his introduction to 'The Postmodern Condition', Lyotard traces the postmodern 'split' in the difference between an affirmative and a reactive response to modern art's devotion to the sublime aesthetic." The affirmative enjoys the dissolution of values and the reactive tries to find a fixed truth when faced with that dissolution of values."(127)

Falconer says that Loe Bersani states that the sublime is a rush of libidinal energy caused when presentation utterly fails. Lyotard's affimative person enjoys this failure and slides into the "noumenal swamp of the body" (128). The self no longer differentiates itself from the world in an ecstatic "spiral beyond cognition" (129). This is the Gnostic mystical position previously described.

Douglas Fogle's article later in Chapmanworld (130) also relates to this paroxysm to induce a sense of the transcendent. He describes work of the Chapmans where the Romantic theology of the artist is replaced with a more scatological (the science of filth) notion of the sacred. He quotes the Chapmans "When our sculptures work they achieve the position of reducing the viewer to a state of moral panic... they're completely troublesome objects." (131) This is like the panic in the work of Anton Artaud with its goal of Gnostic mysticism. Thus the Chapmans' work breaks down moral systems in order to radically change the viewer's perspective. It is a turning into a consumer art product of the work of Gnostic, mystical performance artists.

Some critics, however, think that their work is ill-formed. In "New Art Examiner" Martha Schwendener (132) thinks that "Six Feet Under" rejects the sacred boundaries of the body. "The penises, button holes and labia stuck on the figures are repulsive (like the celebrated big toe of Bataille's essay on the Informe) and yet sexually charged. It is a matter of arrangement and disarrangement. But, as in both Bataille and Deleuge and Gualtari, there is never a logical version of how things should be". She continues that "The Chapmans, obsessed with their own bad-boy aura, have cobbled together, in both their objects and their writings, a hodgepodge of theory that reeks of trendiness." (133)

This trendiness, however, is not a problem for the Chapmans who state that they aim at a bourgeois audience: "We are interested in recuperating every form of terrorism in order to offer the viewer the pleasure of a certain kind of horror, a certain kind of bourgeois convulsion – everybody else visits theme parks." (134)

They try to break down moral and intellectual structures in order to achieve a different perspective. However, they recognise that the Avant-garde no longer has any political power and that their art is just an intellectual game. In other words, they recreate the Gnostic shock of Anton Artaud but it is purely for the purposes of entertainment and has no political or personal transformative power, e.g. their McDonalds based tribal art exhibited at Saatchi Gallery, 2003, with hand carved wooden figures with a tribal masks, holding carved, painted boxes of MacDonalds fries.

This bricolage of consumerism with tribalism ironically combines kitsch with anthropology to make a dubious moral statement that MacDonald's consumerism is a form of atavistic religion. The shock and open art investigation of Picasso's tribal "Les Demoiselles d'Avignon" is replaced with a closed and ironic humour. The Chapmans ironically make secular consumerism into a fetishistic religious option and is more deconstructive of religion. However, like in the work of Hirst, this reduction is a feature of an atheistic Modernism, rather than a postmodern openness to religion.

I think that the Chapmans create a liminality in their work as they represent the world as they see it, however, a real engagement with rights of other religions and ethnic peoples is not shown, just an exhibition of art imperialism and the art consumer system.

The work of the YBAs presents further examples of secular Modern artists who use religious imagery to mock and reject religion. There are numerous examples of this kind of work. Typically the artists engage solely with Christianity as the power that they seek to challenge and to rebel against. It is more destruction as an act of rebellion and freedom than of religious reconstruction. Below are some chronologically listed examples.

Andres Serano's "Piss Christ" 1987, a photograph of crucifix in urine. This was the original work that flirted openly with blasphemy, combining the sacred and the base.

Martin Kippenberrger's "Fred the Frog Rings the Bell" 1990 is a wood carving of a Christ-like frog being crucified, in loincloth, with its tongue sticking out.

Gilbert & George's "Shitty Naked Human World" 1994, a photo-print of a crucifix made out of excrement,

Chris Ofili's "The Holy Virgin Mary" 1996, an African Mary in blue robes surrounded by vaginas from porn magazines and surmounted with elephant dung.

"New Liberty 2006" 1996 by the AES Art Group is an early Muslim cultural example, an edited photo that puts the Statue of Liberty in a Yashmak. It was intended as an image that tried to confront and overcome a phobia but it seems like the artists were attacking "radical" Islamists desire to dominate the Western World.

Maurizio Cattelan's "The Ninth Hour" 1999 is a sculpture of a life-size and lifelike Pope John Paul II felled by a meteorite.

Wes Modes "Prayer Machine II" 2002 is an automated electronic device made of steel, copper and aluminium. It is a device for amplifying prayers. You write a prayer on a slip of paper, drop it in the machine, press a button and the prayer is sent up with smoke as the paper is incinerated.

Sarah Lucas "Christ You Know It Ain't Easy" 2003 was an entire wall painted with an English flag of Saint George and upon which hung a naked, crucified Christ made out of thousands of Marlborough cigarettes.

In 2003 Sharon Lutchman depicted the singer and footballer Victoria and David Beckham as the gods Shiva and Parvati and also David Beckham as a 14th century Icon of Jesus and in 2006 Wayne Rooney (Manchester United footballer) was photographed in a Christ-like crucified pose and painted white with a red cross (the English flag). In 2004 David and Victoria Beckham had waxworks made of them at Madame Tussaud's that were dressed as Joseph and Mary.

"My Mummy Was Beautiful" 2004 at Liverpool Biennial 2004 was Yoko Ono's homage to motherhood made of banners of a woman's breast and crotch being displayed across the city centre and at Liverpool John Lennon Airport. One of Ono's controversial posters sparked complaints and was removed from the deconsecrated St Luke's church on Berry Street.

In 2007 the Grafitti artist Banksy made a mini Stonehenge out of portable toilets in the sacred space at Glastonbury festival. His comment on the work was "A lot of monuments are a bit rubbish, but this really is a pile of crap."

We can also put this work into the context of popular comedy and see that whilst later theatre may have been influenced by this Modern art, the art, in turn, was probably earlier influenced by Monty Python's "Life of Brian" 1979 semi-surreal comedy film about a parallel Messiah figure in the same time and place as Jesus Christ.

In September 2005 the 12 Danish cartoons in the Jyllands-Posten newspaper, most of which depicted the Islamic prophet Muhammad, led to world wide protests and 140 deaths. Around this time Theo van Gogh, a Dutch film-maker, was murdered for making a film portraying violence against women in Islamic societies. Protests in Birmingham also forced the closure of Gurpreet Kaur Bhatti's "Bezhti" 2004, a play about rape and murder in a Sikh Temple.

Some of these works were social comments that it was claimed maintained a degree of respect, however, most used the controversy for advertising and self-promotion – and may have deliberately engineered the controversy.

"Jerry Springer: The Opera" 2006 by Stewart Lee was an openly publicity seeking comedy that was a version of a confessional talk show. In it he presenter looks at ordinary people and ideas of Heaven and Hell, set to a variety of genres of music. Before "Jerry Springer" gets to Adam and Eve, Satan and Jesus (who might be a bit gay) there are trash-talking pole dancers, transvestite hookers, and tap-dancing Klu-Klux-Klansmen in this opera, which is full of swear words and breaks down the high ideals of religion. The play ends with a quote from William Blake's "The Marriage Of Heaven and Hell" where he preaches the mystical position that ultimately everything that lives is holy.

"Jihad: The Musical" 2007 carried on this direction, sending up stock characters of Islamic fundamentalism combining rock and roll and musical-theatre styles with Islamic fundamentalism (including with shiny, pink, burka-clad jihadis).

The film "Religulous" 2009 by Larry Charles was an expose of the ridiculous behaviour of some extreme believers. Comedian Bill Maher makes fun of religious kitsch and extremists but did not address serious theologians.

Rather than just be comedians the YBA artists used religious imagery for gravitas. But even when their work was not full of possible humour they were still not being serious or genuine in their faith. Chris Ofili's "The Upper Room" 1999 – 2002 is large sumptuous semi-abstract paintings of monkeys in the roles of the 12 disciples, with Christ as the chief monkey. This builds on the liminality of his work of the Virgin Mary, "The Holy Virgin Mary" 1996, which combined Aboriginal dots, cuttings from pornographic magazines, African beads, hip-hop and blaxploitation movie imagery.

Sam Taylor-Wood creates glamorous videos and photographs often in semi-religious poses e.g. "Pieta" 2001 a large video projection shown in the Church of All Hallows, London. Sam Taylor-Wood labours to support the draped body of Robert Downey Jr. Her work studies emotion and this pietà becomes a secular icon of exhaustion and distress as she breaks down emotional charged scenarios with a slow-motion study that is both unfamiliar and drained of emotional significance. It is a statement of the challenge to find meaningfulness but it relates not just to religion but to life in general.

YBA artists, however, do not just attack religion, they also expose and utilise genuinely shocking aspects of religion, but this should not be confused with having a genuine religious expression, e.g. Marc Quinn installed a painted, bronze cast of a plastic medical model of a 22-week old foetus in a position of prayer in "Angel" 2007 and installed it in Winchester Cathedral. Whilst not directly criticising the religion by exposing shocking aspects of religion a critique was made. In this instance about the fate of unborn babies in the Catholic church (as they go to Limbo rather than heaven or hell as they have not been given the rites to become members of the church when born). This type of bodily work also links to how there are Catholic relics, with parts and bodies of saints, or decaying bodies of the faithful, in catacombs or on open display in European churches. This is part of tradition and only shocks people outside of those traditions, especially when used in non-religious, non-sacred contexts because no respect is given to the bodies.

A performance artist who fit with both Catholic mortification and the shallow YBA self-aggrandisement in the media is Sebastian Horsley who documented his own crucifixion in a South American Catholic Easter ritual in 1999. However the real celebrity was David Blaine. His 44-day starvation in a suspended perspex box, on the bank of the Thames was a public spectacle that caused far greater public reaction than Hirst's work and his art connected to the life of the majority of people – with the hunger, cold and threat of death. Although the majority would not have recognised it as art.

On the 40th day I looked up to see him enjoying, apparently, the adulation of the crowd gathered beneath him. He was in an elevated position and you had to enter an inner sanctum to see him more closely. He has been hounded by the mob (just as Jesus was) and his sojourn for 44 days was close enough to Jesus' 40 days in the wilderness.

Internet sites debated whether Blaine is a Messiah or anti-Christ but the consensus was that he is a magician who does amazing tricks and feats of physical endurance, that it was all show business. However

Blaine's mental and physical control techniques owe much to fakirs, monks and mystics and Blaine bears a tattoo of Christ that covers his back. And he thanked God at the end of his fast. Whilst this was a media event he also displayed delusions of religious or mystical grandeur. This was pre-modern, fully sincere and non-ironic, curtailed only by his cynical or delusional media manipulation – without the political content or background of early performance artists.

RECENT SPIRITUAL MODERN ARTISTS

The spiritual basis of many Modern artists is a weaker and more general than mysticism as mentioned in our religious definitions. For artists it is often a rejection of forms of religion, replacing them with a belief in some kind of unknown sacred dimension. Because this is weak many Modern spiritual artists continue as part of the commodity system. They and their spirituality are manipulated by corporate forces because it is a consumer spirituality that ignores the political dimension of life. As such it has lost the early transformative power of Modern Avant-garde art and serves as corporate decoration.

There are many examples of this work that has removed itself from a progressive, critical art narrative. And whilst it is not outwardly self-aggrandising (as in the work of the YBAs) it is still firmly part of the commodity system. However, when these kinds of works are placed within societies that have not fully modernised they can still have power to shock and challenge (as in the work of Shirin Neshat) but in a fully modernised society they are merely part of outdated debates.

US artist, Bill Viola, uses ordinary looking people as actors in his short films. He places them in religious tableaux scenes (often scenes from art history) in order to show the universal humanity of the situations (often of life and death, or love and pain) but also to show the spiritual calmness at one remove from all the chaos of the scene. He achieves this by slowing down the movement in the scenes e.g. "Emergence" 2003 is an 11 minute video, inspired by a 15th century fresco by Masolini, where a figure emerges Christ-like from an altar-like tomb that is full of water and is then laid down to rest by 2 figures who resemble Mary and Saint John. This has echoes of his earlier work "The Messenger" Durham Cathedral and his ambitious "Going Forth By Day" Guggenheim Museum 2002 which deal (in main or part) with water, submergence and the passage from one medium into another (a metaphor of the journey from life to the afterlife).

Katharina Fritsch's "St Nicholas" 2002 is a 30 centimetre high polyester statue of a figure in church robes, with an orb and a hat, that is painted bright purple. Like many of her works and numbers of which are arranged in patterns on the floor, making these religiously charged objects into primarily aesthetic, spiritual objects.

Anthony Gormley makes casts of his body as a universal man. These have no clear direction and are awaiting form. This is a surreal, metaphysical and also a nihilistic existentialism. Gormley's 20 metre high "Angel of the North" 1998 is a featureless figure at the side of the A1 road with aeroplane wings. It is a fake totem, quasi-religious aspiring to indefinite higher things, in a spiritual uplift.

Anthony Gormley teamed up with Sidi Larbi Cherkaoui and the Monks from the Shaolin Temple at Sadler's Wells to create a dance collaboration called "Sutra". Gormley and Cherkaoui also joined the dancer and choreographer Akram Khan in "Zero Degrees" 2005. This involved dancing Kathak (the Indian dance associated with the God Krishna) and burning a sculpture that Gormley had made of Khan. Both pieces were a celebration of spirituality.

Similarly the South Asian Dance Company called Akademi created a piece called "Sufi:Zen" 2010 at Furness Abbey, Cumbria. It was a spiritual piece that combined the influences of the Abbey with the mystic traditions of Sufism and Zen Buddhism.

The Indian Jewish artist Anish Kapoor's abstract brightly coloured, large scale, abstract sculptures are also spiritual in their curved shapes, sensual and primary colours. They also have mythic names and play with dualities of space and absence, earth and sky, body and spirit e.g. "Marsayas" 2003, a bright red sculpture which filled the huge Turbine Hall at London's Tate Modern. Marsayas challenged Apollo to a musical dual, lost and was flayed alive for his pride. This statement of the defeat of the Dionysian by the Apollonian suggests that the continued use of Dionysian imagery by artists is part of an YBA type empty, commodified show of spirituality and Gnosticism by an Apollonian art society.

A number of artworks have also arisen from religious societies but these are often secular out of a need for artistic rebellion. As a result they have religious imagery but are part of a process of secularisation (involving women's rights) or spiritualism e.g. Shirin Neshat an Iranian who lives in New York and whose work, like that of the video artist Bill Viola, tends to be mainly spiritual. It is unlike Theo van Gogh's work which was directly political and critical of religion.

Neshat's "Women of Allah" 1993-7 series was photographic portraits of women overlaid by Persian calligraphy and referred to gender and the social, cultural and religious codes of Muslim societies. Neshat's work examines the forces shaping the identity of Muslim women throughout the world, often making stark contrasts between light and dark, male and female. Her "Logic of the Birds" 2001-02, was inspired by the 12th century Persian poet and mystic Farid al-Din Attar. An epic affirmation that true enlightenment comes from within, Attar's tale tells the story of a flock of birds on a quest for meaning. In this synthesis of live performance and video projection, inside Islington's Union Chapel (London) the singer Sussan Deyhim led a silent chorus of men and women as Neshat's cinematic narrative of traditional Muslim women crossing a desert unfolded.

Other artists who link to the spiritual traditions include Cecil Collins, a painter who was an imaginative visionary and believed that art was a metaphysical activity. He was inspired by William Blake and his work was stylised, primitive and figurative, with Celtic influences and a New Age spiritualism (e.g. painting of angels).

This New Age mix of traditions is seen in the work of John Tavener, a composer who creates large-scale pieces for chorus and orchestra. "The Beautiful Names" 2007 is a musical setting for the 99 names of Allah and was performed at the Roman Catholic Westminster

Cathedral. Tavener is Greek Orthodox as he wanted to follow a path and not be New Age and vague (although he is fundamentally New Age as he had a vision of the transcendent unity of all religions after meeting an Apache Indian medicine man). He has used Latin, Sanskrit, Arabic, Aramaic, Greek, American Indian, German and Italian to express something of the divine feminine. He believes in the beauty of nature and in the divine and that the Enlightenment brought a downward path for art. He sees Modernism as masculine and that art has degenerated past even humanity. He fails to see that his New Age vision is just one half of the Modernist vision.

Another artists who believes in this unity but who is more critical of religion is John Latham. His "God Is Great (No. 2)" 1991 involved the cutting in half of a Talmud, a Bible and a Koran then putting them together again, but divided by a sheet of silicon. The work suggested that the religions are ultimately identical at a deep level. However, his process of deconstruction and reconstruction marks a beginning of Postmodern Religious Art.

RECENT SOCIO-RELIGIOUS MODERN ARTISTS

Another trend in recent artists is to allude to religious imagery purely for the purposes of personal and social commentary. This involves an exploration and descriptive reportage of everyday life. This can be seen as part of a faux scatological breakdown of the art's exclusivity by turning everyday incidents into high art but it remains within the gallery system.

Work by Mark Wallinger, tends to be mainly Christian but is also more about observations of British Society and of Britishness. Mark Wallinger's video installation "Threshold to the Kingdom" refers to the arrival of immigrants to the United Kingdom at the London City international airport. The doors open and the often bewildered travelers arrive and walk towards the camera. Choral music is playing and the allusion is to souls arriving in Heaven. There is a parallel between the judgment awaiting at the customs gates and the gates of the after-life and the work questions some deeper reality and judgment. Like much of Wallinger's work he draws parallels between traditional and modern British beliefs and actions and highlights the absurdity and yet necessity of these in a society of diverse race, culture and class.

The Singh Twins, Amrit and Rabindra, use traditional, colourful, decorative, illustrative techniques from in Indian miniature painting to produce vibrant, detailed paintings. The fusion of Sikh and Western influences is a vehicle for witty political and social commentary, critically challenging stereotypes and narrow perceptions of heritage, identity, materialism, the cult of celebrity and politics.

'All Hands on Deck' 1997, was created in response to being criticised for the style of their work being too Eastern. In the painting the artists' family prepares a wedding feast in the front yard outside their home. It is painted in the style of traditional Persian miniatures, framed within a large, decorative, gazebo. The extended family is in modern dress is involved in traditional cooking activities in a rejection of Western Individualism, symbolised by the Union Jack cardboard box in a pile of rubbish. Other works include "From Zero To Hero" 2002, with the footballer and pop star David and Victoria Beckhams as the New Royal Family and 'Nineteen Eighty Four' 1998, which depicts the Indian Government's storming of the Sikh Golden Temple in 1984. These works are more an exploration of identity (begun by artists in the 1960's) than an expression of religious belief.

Nathan Coley's "Camouflage Church" 2006 is a half-size cardboard model of a church painted in gaudy stripes as an exploration and questioning of how architecture is invested with meaning in public space. It was exhibited at the Turner Prize in the Tate Liverpool along with Coley's "There Will Be No Miracles Here" 2006 is a neon sign spelling those words, on scaffolding, in a wood. Again, religious imagery is used but more as an architectural and sociological exploration.

Again, the artist Mitra Tabrizian is an Iranian-British photographer who creates elaborate photographic tableau that looks at the rise of corporate culture, and at themes of nomadism, migration and homeland, e.g. her photograph "Tehran" 2006 that shows a run down residential area where the crowds of people are struggling in their traditional society, as more concerned with a broad social study.

Our final example, Valerie Mrejen's "Dieu (God)" 2007, exhibited in Tate Modern, is a video where eight Israelis recall the incidents that led them to abandon their Orthodox Jewish faith. This shows how religious elements are used as a way to make a secular study of society and faith.

NEW MODERNISTS (TECHNO MODERN)

Instead of just accepting complicity with the commodity system there are also artists who propose that technology can be used as a way to fight the consumer Spectacle. Marshall McLuhan argues that the structure of new technology might provide a way for community effort to oppose the oppressive Spectacle and "hyperreality". McLuhan was influential on Baudrillard and wrote on how he believed that the media revolution had led to a decentralising of the world into virtual communities and that the structure of computing meant more for social and psychological change than its contents (as borne out by social networking sites such as Facebook). The structure leads to a high degree of audience participation and non-linear thinking that can bring communities around the world together. Ward, however, points out that community interaction is not necessarily harmonious, with the media used by competing multi-national corporations and different political and religious factions (137).

Ward discusses Mark Poster's argument that as national borders dissolve, and new ways to communicate are introduced, so also central authority dissolves and the private consumer becomes simultaneously the public producer. The internet provides new ways for communities to form and these virtual, on-line communities can be used politically (138). However, these virtual communities can also bring a diversification of consumer groups that lead to less centralised, politically weaker, challenges to abuses of power (139).

Socially interactive world-wide communication is also a Dionysian use of Apollonian technology. This breaks down the subject-object distinctions in a pantheistic way although it is also becoming a method of surveillance and control by the ruling elite – just as the printing press initially freed people from single, Catholic, interpretations of scripture but was later used by the elite for controlling people through the mass media spectacle.

This homogenisation and control of the internet and telecommunications is another example of why modern technological progress might not provide the political strategy to overcome centralised abuses of power.

A mystical dimension has been ascribed to the internet as, like in mystical experience, the connections exist in an immaterial space and over vast distances. And this new Techno-mysticism holds that instead of nature being dominated by technology, technology is part of nature. Techno-shamanism it is a loose term to cover artists who integrate nature, spirituality and technology. Some of its followers even try to synthesise completely by incorporating cyborg, robotic parts into the body.

Stelarc (Stelios Arkadiou) is a performance artist who focuses on extending the capabilities of the human body. His performances are centred around the concept that the human body is obsolete. They often involve robotics or modern technology integrated with his body, such as a cell-cultivated surgical ear attached to his arm. In another performance his body was hooked up to electrodes and connected to the internet so that a worldwide audience could remotely control him by muscle stimulators. This discipline owes as much to Hindu monks as it does to live art (with early works by Stelarc involving himself being suspended by hooks through his skin in a deliberate allusion to the practices of Hindu monks).

Another example of this combination of technology and mysticism is by Mariko Mori who used Buddhist iconography in his projected environments e.g. "Pure Land" 1996-98. Here a photographic construction of a Buddhist deity mingles with computer designed avatars that fly on clouds. His later work "Wave UFO" 1999-2002 had a silver, paisley shaped spaceship shaped room that viewers could climb up into. Inside lights and shapes were projected. The artist is trying to express through the work is the idea that we're part of a whole and also that that part is a whole. His aim was to make personal transformation through art. He sees himself and his art as evolving. In addition Mariko does not see the spiritual as being more important than the material. Both are of equal value. (140)

A group movement that also employs ambient environments with religious imagery is Reverend Matthew Fox's "Techno Cosmic Mass". This is a bricolage of art, a kind of religious rave and ritual theatre. Fox is an ex-Catholic Priest who proposes that religion has an inner mystic core: "The best hope for our planet is a recovery of a living, mystical cosmology. That can happen as we let the modern era recede, by incorporating a celebration of the mystical along with a celebration of the analytical" (141)

Fox opposes a Newtonian, materialist, passive observance of life with a perspective of Quantum physics. His movement from "the Newtonian parts-mentality to the deep ecumenism of an era of the Cosmic Christ in all world religions" assumes that the deeper truth is the Cosmic Christ and rejects the traditional, anthropomorphic religions in favour of a Modernist abstract mysticism (which he falsely characterises as being postmodern).

"The Techno Cosmic Mass is a post-modern worship experience which is rooted in Western liturgical tradition and integrates ecstatic music and dance, urban shamanism, multimedia imagery and Eastern and indigenous spiritual elements. Each new Techno Cosmic Mass is an experiment in bringing together people of diverse ages, faiths and cultures in shared prayer which holds true to our ancestral traditions, respects and honours our differences, and highlights our common bonds." Techno Cosmic Mass leaflet (142).

The Techno Cosmic Mass is a simulacra it is a reconstruction of religious systems but they have an underlying mysticism as a shared, serious, genuine core. A typical Techno Cosmic Mass is a room "full of flashing lights, candles, screens projecting images of galaxies and people and nature." The shadows of dancers (behind white screens backlit with orange lights) are seen and there are also fire dancers to connect with natural elements (143).

The monthly events "are multicultural, post-denominational worship services, drawing hundreds of supporters" "to dance, sing, chant, grieve, pray and celebrate". "It's a concoction of mysticism, feminism and environmentalism stirred by the traditions and rituals of Christians, Buddhists, Jews, American Indians, Wiccans, pagans, you name it – forging one big happy cosmic family"

Fox's work is both anti-corporation and pro-environment but also firmly linked to commodity structures with The Friends of Creation Spirituality, Inc. presentation of multimedia resources live performances, public forums and rituals to support its University (144).

Other Techno Shamanism clubs tended to have Pagan or Eastern religious themes, e.g. in the UK "Escape from Samsara", "Kundalini", "Tribalism" and "Planet Angel". These clubs contained group dancing, visual projections and immersive lighting, however, the emphasis in these clubs was also on hallucinogens and Ecstasy. To create an atmosphere to induce states of trance the clubs have very loud, techno, tribal rhythms as well as areas for people to "chill out" and relax. This relates back to the use of L.S.D. in the 1960's counter-culture as a consumer mysticism.

Other party goers take the ideology behind their clubbing seriously and treat events as being almost pilgrimages. Every August about 30,000 artists, anarchists, a new Age thinkers travel to take part in "The Burning Man Festival" in Nevada's Black Rock Desert. Elaborate structures and artworks are built and after the giant constructed man is burned they are then dismantled at the end of the festival. In 2003 the theme was beyond belief. It was an attempt to go beyond the dogmas, creeds and metaphysics of religion to the primal, immediate experience from whence faith arises. The actual wooden man for burning was built about a giant Temple that was based on a Hindu Mandala pattern. This follows the Carnivalesque of Bhaktin as a way to break down structures in celebratory parties.

The above artists all show how that whilst the integration of technology into art may have a political use it has been ideologically led (in art) by mysticism with its unification of nature and technology. The actual, moral and political use of the new technology has been more direct - with blogs, facebook, youtube, websites and twitter as the prime "artistic" mediums. However these broadcast mediums may not have been considered artistic because their use is too narrative and didactically political.

POSTMODERN MULTICULTURALISM

The increased access to internet technology leads to greater voices for marginalised groups so that they can create their own communities. Technology can also be used by communities to try and overcome oppressive structures and in a postmodern context community opposition will of necessity be multicultural due to the diversity of voices that technology facilitates. Ironically this postmodernism is dependent on the modern technology.

In his introduction to "Documenta XI" Okuwi Enwezor called for a more inclusive, global art that addressed marginalized ethnic groups and he viewed Ground Zero metaphorically, as a new starting point and a space for cultures other than those of the USA to grow and engage in debate. The dead certainties of colonialism and Modernism have come to a crisis point and Enwezor believes that Muslim and other cultures are contesting this space. He thought that interaction with marginal cultures in a montage has critical content and presents the last major challenge to Western consumer culture (145).

In fact, Linda Woodhead and Paul Heelas, editors of "Religion in Modern Times", already argued that there is a widespread suspicion of grand narratives in postmodern thinking but dominance of the grand narrative of secularisation (that religion was affected by Modernity in the direction of decline) was unquestioned in much of the twentieth century. Now a sacralization model has arisen due to evidence of religious vitality in much of the world (excluding Northern Europe). The revolution in Iran, mobilization of Islam, rise of religious nationalism in the Middle East and former USSR and the rise of Hindu militancy in India and Sri Lanka, shows that religion plays a role in ethnic and national identity (146).

Patrice Pavis, the editor of The Intercultural Performance Reader, worries that the appearance of a global culture is not democratic but is really the subsuming of all individual cultures under the dominant West (consumerism) (147). The only way to ensure democracy is to ensure that there is a diversity of voices and not a dominance by a single Modernist mystical or atheistic viewpoint.

Artists have explored the difficulty of maintaining this diversity. Erika Doss writes about Guillermo Gomez Pena's work in her study of Twentieth-Century American art. She says that he explored how ethnic identities are constructed and commodified as stereotypes for media consumption. Doss says that Gomez Pena thinks that dominant cultures appropriate cultural forms but no control is given back to the other cultures. His suggestion is to use a syncretic model where identities are not sharply defined and are used as a way of critiquing political authority and social oppression (148).

Gomez Pena describes some of his ideas of such a syncretic model. His mission is "to create new, hybrid ritual capable of expressing our fears and contradictions, or existential malaise, our political uncertainties and trans- or inter-cultural complexities (149)." These hybrid identities are a combination of parts but have no fixed essence. The hybrid personas that he creates eg: pregnant nuns, holy gang members, crucified political activists, curio shop shamans, and pop cultural Madonnas appear to be both religious and anti-religious.

Gomez Pena thinks that in postmodernity, religion is inevitably intertwined with pop and mass culture but that powerful political and religious symbols can be completely changed when put into new contexts. Such work inevitably implies political consequences because of the adverse reactions that it might generate and in Mexico this led to his work being trashed by religious fundamentalists outraged at his use of the Virgin Mary in 1983. (150)

Gomez Pena's political strategy is to constantly question and reinvent his identity (151). This challenges authority but his performances are an exotic, entertaining carnival, freak-show or museum, where guns and sex mix together with cultural artefacts. These different combinations gave no real progression and felt very superficial even though they pretended to make an important political statement.

Gomez-Pena's "Temple of Confessions" is described in Temple of Confessions: Mexican Beasts and Living Santos. It was an interactive performance based exhibition designed to examine public perceptions of Mexican-American culture. Mexican religious and cultural images were combined with pre-Colombian, colonial and pop icons. These were placed in a chapel-like environment (that included altars) and the artists performed ritual tasks within these environments (at various US museums through 1994).

The artists were encased in glass exhibition cabinets that contained words in neon, paraphenalia and living creatures (cockroaches, crickets and iguana). The smell of incense come from below temple icons. These icons were borderland, hybrid "saints" painted on black velvet in faux gilt frames.

Items of kitsch such as a ceramic Bart Simpson, an oversized hamburger bank, and a Day of the Dead sugar skull, were all sanctified in the temple space. In the centre was a taxidermied chicken in a noose over a body bag (marked with the initials of the immigration authority) (152).

An actress and a dancer, posed as "nuns" (one pregnant with tattoos of a gangster and the other a dominatrix with a goatee beard) and chanted religious songs. They used their veils to clean the display boxes, the body bag and visitors' shoes (153).

Visitors were invited to contribute their "confessions", of how they viewed Mexican culture, to the artists. The public expressed sexual desire, hatred, contempt and fear and the artists accepted this without judgement. About a third of the visitors kneeled to confess. Visitors were also encouraged to light candles beneath the paintings of hybrid saints and to leave personal offerings, such as photos, tampons, coins and flowers (154).

The space was a kind of mythic theatre between church, stylised trading post, ethnographic shop, funfair and cheap museum. This space allowed the coexistence of multiple perspectives and reactions (155) and where people could reflect on their own racist attitudes.

Gomez-Pena says that irreverent humour is at the core of Mexican art and is a political strategy. He uses this as a way to deal with heavy issues without causing too much negative reaction. However it also runs the risk of trivialising issues as people expect spirituality to be very serious (156).

Gomez-Pena says that he is strongly influenced by Catholicism despite his conscious rejection of formalized religion.

His political strategy is to be a border citizen who constantly questions and reinvents his identity (157). This challenges authority but I think that the border-crossing is a liminal state and that Gomez-Pena is happy to stay between borders and does not make a space for a genuine religious revelation.

Although he allows religious sentiments to appear he does not appear to encourage them as genuine worship. This is part of the problem for a postmodern culture as whilst the voices of minority groups are promoted religion is still rejected as being too volatile or as being inimical to postmodern thinking.

As a result his work is more intercultural than interreligious and is not creating a space for people to create their own religion, so much as their own culture.

The cultural, political hybrids fit what Michael Newman describes as the postmodern movement called the Trans-avantgarde. This work is without avant-garde political intention other than to confuse symbolic expectations and break-down historical imagery. Newman points out that whilst the avant-garde had specific political purposes the trans-avant-garde just wish to break down rationality (158). However, in the face of knowing they have no political effect they are futile.

Bonito Oliva and Frederick Jameson are theorists who argue that a superficial mixing of cultures has no political role and creates a depthless society. Bonito Oliva argued that art now operates like a game without political challenge. He proposed that the historic avant-garde was involved in a critical, dialectical progression of reuniting opposites but in contrast to this the Trans-avantgarde (founded in Italy in 1979) rejected ideological progress, preferring to imitate and fragment various historical art forms. Instead of a expressing a grand avant-garde synthesis, artists just made an

130

eclectic use of diverse imagery. Figurative elements are joined with abstract elements, and historical art images are linked with popular culture but the appropriation is without cohesion, synthesis or political direction and is just another marketable commodity (159).

Sayre notes how Transavant-garde art can have the appearance of a taboo narrative and subverts the split between high and low culture but it is without Avant-garde political intention other than to confuse symbolic expectations. He suggests that Transavant-garde art is just another marketable commodity. The appropriation is liminal, without political direction (160). Gomez Pena's hybrids seem to be just one more example of these experiences. They are multicultural and do not allow religion a genuine space as religion is mixed with secular icons in a breakdown that is without leadership to say that the religious aspect is still genuine.

POSTMODERN RELIGIOUS ART

A position which has diverse perspectives without collapsing into complete deconstruction because it also involves religious faith. This position is in opposition to spiritual Modernism and to Hirst's postmodern nihilism is postmodern religion.

Anthony Vidler is the Professor and Chairman of the Department of Art History at the University of California, he argues that the uncanny is described in Freud's 1919 essay and is a modern notion that grew out of Burke's idea of the sublime. It is a terror that arises from the invasion of an alien presence into the domestic sphere. These anxieties and fears also give rise to a feeling of estrangement, where the familiar (homely) suddenly becomes unfamiliar (unhomely) (161). The house pretends to offer security but opens itself to terror and horror, as in a haunted house.

I propose that the sublime is invoked in the liminal because the breakdown of linguistic/conceptual structures gives them fear. This creates either flight and a reconfiguration/rebirth in new, oppositional structures (such as religious systems) or in a Modernist mystical transcendence.

The Surrealists used shocking images in order to create the uncanny as a liminal state between dream and waking. The postmodernists inherited the Surrealists' combination of breaking down structures and creating symbolic narratives. Postmodernists use the uncanny to destabilise our views by introducing Other political and social beings. Vidler thinks, however, that as previous avant-garde expressions of the Other had little effect on the political landscape so new (transavant-garde) expressions are known to be ineffectual and to use them with this knowledge is to trivialise social and political action (162).

However, I think that postmodern mixing of religious styles can take on scary, uncanny dimension that makes them politically explosive. They can create a fear of reactions of the Other – in the form of terrorism that will only stop, following a renegotiation with the Other, – to create an economic equality that might stop the Other from violently reacting to a liberal, postmodern presentation of religion.

To differentiate this from Modernist Avant-garde provocation there also needs to be a genuine religious element. Brian Walsh (Christian Reformed Chaplain to the University of Toronto) claims in his web article Derrida and the Messiah: The Spiritual Face of Post-modernity, that because Modernism linked to humanism and to spirituality so postmodernism might re-link to the religious. "The problem is that "the end of religion" and "the death of God" are modernist, Enlightenment dogmas. They are the ultimate conclusion of the modernist blind faith in human autonomy."(163)

Derrida's view of Messianicity is not necessarily religious but is a rupture in expectation. Faith in universal justice and in rational systems is not founded on rationality. It is spontaneous and quasi automatic. It is a faith in the Messianic uprooting from dogmatism and it allows a space for universal rationality and political democracy by looking to new faith perspectives. However, it never allows those perspectives to be realised for as soon as one appears it is expectant of the next (164). In contrast the Chora is an empty space, a desert and a Nothing, it is a realm of possibility in opposition to the actual revealing of religion. (165)

Derrida views religion as Abrahamic (related to Jewish, Christian and Muslim faiths) and sees Messianicity as not necessarily religious but as a rupture in horizons of expectation: "First name: the messianic, or messianicity without messianism. This would be the opening to the future or to the coming of the other as the advent of justice, but without horizon of expectation and without prophetic prefiguration." (166)

Walsh suggests that Derrida's non-determinate Messianicity is a weak Messianism that will not claim too much for itself. Derrida's belief in Messianicity is part of human expectation of a Messiah that cannot be fulfilled in a determinate, un-deconstructible way. Walsh suggests that the concept of Messianicity needs a determinate Messiah (perspective) for it to be fulfilled. (167)

I suggest that this tension between deconstruction and a constructive meaning could be resolved in provisional ideas of Messiahs that allow space for "divine intervention" and Victor E. Taylor's idea of the Parasacred (given in Para/Inquiry: Postmodern Religion and Culture) is a way to explain how belief can arise out of postmodern liminality.

Taylor gives an example of the Parasacred as being graveyard symbols that are almost completely areligious. Images of cars carved on to granite tombstones are an expression of a person's hopes in the context of death and of their gravest fears and doubts, but "unlike the Holy Cross, the Virgin Mary, an angel or other religious images," the car links to an ultimate that is "without resolution and without promise." The images offer no redemption or solace, only parasacrality. "The car opens the "Ultimate" to a "plural ultimate" that is "para", "alongside, beside, and a subsidiary of the sacred." (168)

Taylor sees the representation of a footballer as more truthful, pious and genuine as it recognises the failure of the overtly religious and provides its own parody that suggests the inadequacy of such representations. I suggest that such representations are a genuine expression of love and grieving. And I think that it is the same with postmodern religious expression are unable to be fully religious but are still full of passion and purpose and give room for making a religious wish or prayer. There is no attempt to find grand narratives or an aesthetic, transcendent or political unity (like Schelling or Hegel's). There is just a semi-ironic faith in a higher power that can overcome problems that the believer is experiencing.

Postmodern religion would be just a simulation of religions, taking historical images of images of religion. These are not used as dogmatic pictures of reality, they are provisional myths that allow for creative revelation. The mixing of religious forms would not be seen as a parody or blasphemy but rather as a parasacrality, where the institutional religions are deconstructed but are then reconstructed as individual expressions. Postmodern Religious Art might facilitate a revelation that can break through the Simulation of reality.

Walsh also thinks that the postmodern action of deconstruction (involving a breaking down of dogmas) provides a model for toleration and co-operation, not just a nihilistic rejection of absolutes. As such there is a moral system in both postmodernism and deconstruction which aims at truth, justice social cohesion and unity. But this system is never determinate, just embodied in the act of deconstruction.

From the above characteristics it should not be assumed that Postmodern Religious Art has depth. It does not produce a religious sentiment but rather at a postmodern religious sentiment. It is a superficial veneer and a set of provisional mythic, anthropological, moral and Messianic doctrines that are subject to revision. However, although Postmodern Religious Art has the form of commodity, irony and the secular, space is made for the uncanny and the parasacred to break through to non-commodifiable, sincere and sacred sentiments.

Postmodern Religious Art is a rejection of the central perspectives of mysticism or spirituality that arose in Modern art thought.

It is a return to faith but not with characteristics of pre-modern religion. It is concerned with the common practice of experimental ritual, artistic, musical, fashion and architectural activities put into a bricolage of superficial consumerism, semi-irony and a lack of a single meaning. It is mainly A2 in our schema but with elements of A1, B1 and B2.

Important to the debate on whether postmodernism is just part of Modernism and Late Capitalism is the belief that "Postmodern Religious Art" is a superficial consumer veneer over Modernism. It does not completely replace Modernism. Modernism is seen as the core perspective over which faith is a veneer.

The movement is part of a response to the failure of the Modernist Avant-Garde. It is an appeal to Divine Intervention to overcome moral oppression. The Divine Intervention is through the purchasing, consumption and creative rearrangement of religious rituals, beliefs and artefacts. The only way of escape from this selfish consumerism is for God to liberate us.

The theology is "a communal practice of creative religious consumerism". There is no central belief other than in the structure of the constant creation of new combinations of religions in a semi-ironic hope that Divine Intervention will occur and for each individual to have their own miracles, healings, visions and revelations.

Traditional religions cater for people who don't like experimentation but a postmodern religious climate will give people options on how to combine, liberalise and change traditional views. Such work implies political consequences because of the adverse reactions that it might generate from fundamentalists.

It is not an attempt to found a new religion (pre-modern) but to create conditions whereby other people feel free to create their own religions. They can create their own narratives and then from this create their own icons (commodities) and rituals.

Postmodern Religious Art is not just an object it is a belief system and set of ritual experiences. It is about both consumer and objects in modes of consumption, creatively adapting and constructing both.

Postmodern Religious Art is a theology of communal practice where art and consumerism are important elements of a search for religious meaning and where the uniting factor is the process of seeking truth rather than any actual truth claims (this is a feature of work which adapts different visual and musical art forms in different expressions).

A de-essentialized, constructive postmodernism (united by a consumerist theology of communal practice) will direct life and alter patterns of consumption, creating positive (but limited) changes. However, initially, postmodern religion would create political unrest and condemnation because of responses from non-commodified (i.e. fundamentalist) religious groups.

Commodified Religion is not just shops selling Orthodox and Catholic crucifixes, icons, prayer-beads, postcards, posters, olive wood figures, t-shirts, cups, satchels, carpets. It is the whole society's approach to the religious faith. How it picks ands selects whichever faith it likes without any deep commitment (as opposed to people being born into a traditional faith or a new faith converting believers into it).

Postmodern religious consumerism can be criticised for being idolatrous by mixing religious imagery, but it is only idolatrous to those who make the religious forms (clothing, music, imagery, ritual) into idols and do not focus on their religious function.

In fact, Woodhead and Heelas say that Rodney Start, argues in favour of religious consumerism (169), as in a pluralist economy, the specialist religion can cater for special needs and tastes of specific market segments. This leads to a higher degree of participation as religions meet the needs of a greater number of consumers.

However, there is also concern that religions are being trivialised and will lose their transformative power. Although Moore says that a benefit of this is that the market also provides a framework for religious debate and relations that were less tolerant in earlier cultures (170). This democracy of religion is produced by enabling free choice, which, in turn, requires education about the various options.

Patrice Pavis, the editor of The Intercultural Performance Reader, worries that interculturalism is just an appropriation of other cultures, e.g. foods, music, clothing and ritual styles, by a dominant culture that will destroy the cultures which it assimilates (171). This appropriation is where one culture just takes the other culture and uses it for its own ends (172). The appearance of a global culture is not democratic but is really the subsuming of all individual cultures under the dominant West (consumerism) (173).

The production of challenging iconic works creates a postmodern religious climate which gives people options on how to combine, liberalise and change traditional views. Such work inevitably implies political consequences because of the adverse reactions that it might generate from fundamentalists. Years after I began writing these ideas and exhibiting my work the 2005 Danish Jyllands-Posten Cartoons have provided this – but they were from a mocking perspective.

Benjamin R. Barber, in his bestseller, "Jihad vs McWorld : Terrorism's Challenge to Democracy", proposes that the modern world and global culture is being torn apart by two forces, those of economics and those of national/religious fundamentalism. He also thinks that both forces are inherently totalitarian and inimical to democracy which must be based on active civic participation.

Barber suggests that the free market is non-democratic but I suggest that it is just that the control of the market is by monopolies that do not allow the postmodern nature of the market to appear. They control unfair trade tariffs and countries subjected to economic injustice by the first world reject political modernism as a viable alternative. Thus fundamental forms of religion are adopted, rather than liberal, democratic religious forms. I suggest that political democracy will follow if economic democracy is created.

The work has an avant-garde transformative effect on traditional cultures and then a superficial postmodern religious effect on those cultures once they are modernised.

The work is almost an update on the exploration of feminst and gay identity art of the 1970's, only it includes faith in divine intervention and is not just using shock as a tactic for political or personal transformation. Artists exploring issues of racial identity had been making this kind of work, e.g. Gomez-Pena (as described) and earlier by Sun Ra, the black musician, who made a cult film "Space Is The Place" 1974 about taking African-Americans back to a heavenly world away from the white overseer. This mix of science fiction, jazz and art is part of the creation of a myth in opposition to white domination and is a form of Gnostic rejection of the enslaving Demi-urge.

And Faisal Abdu'Allah, whose "The Last Supper" 1995 has two images of men and women, where they are dressed in one in African Muslim clothes and in the other in modern clothes. The work shows the similarity to the disciples of people in the African Muslim countries, and also how those peoples are now transposed into a modern, secular persona, neither of which fits their identity fully. The religious dimension of these works, however, are secondary to the broader cultural and racial challenge. Postmodern Religious Art brings religion back as a primary concern.

However, the balance between irony and sincere belief in pluralist religious art is difficult to achieve if you are not to reduce all religions to a vague spirituality or an ecumenical mysticism. There is also the difficulty that when artists engage with issues of religious diversity they revert to atheistic irony.

You enter Lionello Borean's "Plug 'n' Pray" website www.plug-pray.org and it has the image of a normal computer shop. A salesman in a suit and tie has religious symbols on his left side and on his right are colour coded computer boxes with symbols of various religions on their covers. The opening page has a trademark of the Holy Corporation and the statement "Getting converted has never been so easy." All the products are lined up like an educational resource and have the appearance of being professionally designed, with specifications stating that the product is easy to install, has manuals and has an online help system. The scene would be completely without irony apart from the title "START YOUR OWN HOLY WAR! Change their religion with "Plug 'n' Pray"". These add-ons for computers can be used to help in worship, but "their" (in the appeal to "change their religion") refers in an aggressive way to unbelievers.

When you click on "why do you need this", the idea is given that it is so that the user is able to change religion quickly to suit any social or political occasion. This is treating the religion as a lifestyle option. A critical point is implied, that the different religions all share the fact that they attach labels to themselves, almost like corporate branding. The boundary between a religion and a corporation is thus blurred and we can see elements of corporate branding in religion and of aggressive religious fervour in corporate marketing.

Details from Christian, Jewish and Muslim kits are advertised with Buddhist and Hindu options also available at a smaller size. They are advertised as having all the details of religious and cultural habits, fully illustrated in audio and visual files. The packs include cut out and wear cards to explain symbols and attires and the emphasis is on being able to customise the religion to meet your needs. The site continues with each religious symbol translated into a corporate identity of standard lime green logo and text on a white backdrop. This further standardises the religion as a commodity. The work appears to fully commodify religion in an electronic and Global age, but when you go to purchase the products you find that they are not available.

The site appears sincere but is just an ironic satire whereas postmodern religions should maintain transformative possibilities. Such semi-ironic religious commodities would give space for a non-simulated, non-commodifiable change/effect in peoples' lives.

This process or reducing religion to a commodity as a process of critique was turned back upon itself with examples like "The Brick Testament" 2005 by Rev Brendan Powell Smith who made scenes from the Bible out of Lego in order to make them more accessible. This was fixed to one tradition and was for narrative purposes only (rather than being part of a religious worship or transformation). It was also reminiscent of and contemporary with John Cake and Darren Neave copying into Lego famous artworks (such as Damien

Hirst's shark in formaldehyde ("The Physical Impossibility of Death in the Mind of Someone Living").

Another example of traditional, pre-modern religious believers using modern art or technology is Tinariwen. These Saharan Muslim Musicians dress in traditional clothes and for them the separation from culture and religion is not as sharp as in modern society.

However, Postmodern Religious Art is not about reducing religious figures into consumers, e.g. in 2004 the photographer David Gilroy, as part of a residency at my "Inter-religious Art Flat" project, made montage images of the Virgin Mary eating a burger in "Ranch house" 2004 and Saint Peter shopping in "Hitchens" 2004. Both images are set around the seaside resort of Morecambe – drawing parallels to lonely old men and teenage mothers. A few years later the graffiti artist Banksy sprayed images with a similar idea, e.g. "Christ With Shopping Bags" which shows Christ crucified whilst holding shopping bags. These works comment about the ordinariness of these figures and suggests that they are people and not just divine. This reduction was only half of the objective of Postmodern Religious Art, the other half being their use of part of a new form of belief and worship.

In contrast to the Techno Shaman clubs there are examples of Gay clubs with a religious theme; "Heaven", "Salvation", "Sanctuary" and (on the Asian gay scene) "Club Kali". These clubs are purely superficial and pay limited reference to the religious traditions at most they use kitsch visuals of the tradition. There is an interest in alcohol, dancing and sexual encounter in these clubs. The male clubs also have a hind of sado-masochistic leather boy image. An artist who connected with this and explored the use of bizarre fashion, make-up and clubbing as art was Leigh Bowery in the 1980's. However an artist linking to the disco and rock scene in a more postmodern religious manner is the Reverend Ethan Acres. He presents a bricolage of semi-ironic kitsch religious imagery and is a licensed preacher who uses his Highway chapel (a converted caravan) to conduct weddings and uses art in his performance services.

The programme for his London Mission (17-26 October 2002) states that "Revd Acres plays on the history of the holy fool, fusing the flamboyant and the humorous with a deep and genuine spirituality." His messages use a combination of Christian and Jungian imagery, as well as images taken from popular culture, such as Peter Pan and Kiss Rock music "The Guise of Satan" fa projects, London, 2002.

Acres has an evangelical Christian religious preaching style but an underlying philosophy that is a joining of the sacred and the secular (though is not multicultural) in favour of a mystical reconciliation of opposites. In PANopticon" Tate Modern 2002, a performance in the Turbine Hall at Tate Modern he dressed as a preacher, dragging a fellow performer behind him. The fellow performer was dressed as a shadow and was attached by their ankles to his ankles. To conclude Revd Acres rolled down the Turbine Hall with the Shadow and then shed his priestly robes and skipped away dressed in an undersized Peter Pan costume (the shadow side having apparently disappeared). Here he symbolically put his light side and shadow side together.

Revd Acres uses kitsch and creates mythological photographs as a form of surreal symbolism. This use appears superficial and ironic, as do his preachings and services. However he conveys a serious message and as such his work is parasacred. Revd Acres presents a simulation of religious life but also encourages people to enter into religious sentiments that they do not normally believe in. This creates the possibility for them of a genuine religious expression.

Revd Acres' links to music were shown in "Snake in the Grass" 2002, a performance made at the Eve Club in London's West End. This is the UK's only dance floor, with 1970's style disco light floor tiles and a bikini clad girl danced seductively around him. He placed his robes over the girl and came out of his robes dresses as a serpent. Again the emphasis was to accept the opposites. Revd Acres' tattoos and rock and roll influences make him appear as if at home in a gay disco. This union and his non-dualistic message show that his work relates to a mystical breakdown of traditional religious moral identities.

Works like Shilpa Gupta's "Blessed-bandwidth" 2003, are both multi-faith and deep as it is tied with a new faith perspective. You enter her website, www.blessed-bandwidth.net, and see Hindu and Indian derived religious imagery. On the site Gupta urges you to "get Blessed and Feel Secure", an ironic reference to the security of internet connections. As you move the mouse around the site a robed, monk-like figure carrying a rifle appears. The robes are combat camouflaged, suggesting a link between religion and military rule. You are also warned that you are being watched by the state but this appears as a playful, rather than a serious, statement.

You can "log on" and "immerse" yourself into the blessed bandwidth, implying a full experience, with gold and cerise circles giving feelings of heavenly peace. Four options are then given – "verification" "get blessed", "download" and "library". To enter each option you must choose from Hindu, Muslim, Sikh, Christian or Buddhist religions in Mumbai. A picture of the holy site comes up with a colourful image of architecture or a deity from the religion in a band across the top of the screen, and information about its importance. Gupta then states that she took an Internet Network Cable and Requested blessings from various faith leaders, for peace and happiness, to whoever connects to the bandwidth of that cable.

To see images of how the cables are blessed and verified in different religions you are asked to comply with religious observances e.g. remove footwear, cover your head etc. In the process of verification you see videos play of rituals performed in a Hindu Temple, Muslim Mausoleum, Sikh Gurdwara, Christian Church, Art of Living Holy Centre and a Buddhist Temple. There is a connection made between all the faiths by virtue of the same style of presentation of similar ritual processes for the blessing of the computer wires.

At the "Get Blessed" section of the site each religion had images of their Gods, e.g. the Hindu elephant God, Ganesh, the same coloured balls and step-by-step process for receiving a blessing. "1. Sit straight, don't lean. 2. Bend Slowly Forward. Concentrate. 3.Now touch your forehead to the computer screen on Spot X." I followed these instructions and then the computer pop-up said "would you like to certify the Blessing?" I clicked "OK" and then a download page to printout appeared with this text "this object has been blessed such that it will bring peace and happiness wherever it stands". I felt a subjective connection to this being a religious object although I was not convinced that anything religious had occurred but had a small sense that something of meaning and significance might have occurred.

Heidi Reitmaier, External Events Officer at the Tate Modern, notes how Gupta suggests that the "real" nature of the blessing received is dependent on the belief of the user. Reitmaier says that Gupta's work proposes a series of spiritual options without definite solutions. It is non-prescriptive and facilitates questioning. Reitmaier also suggests that there is "a sense of flippancy and disregard were it not for the more profound questions raised about the present status of ancient faiths" (174).

Reitmaier says that the site invites a "subjective, highly personal, incoherent and accumulative" interaction but also asks the user to reflect on their own interests in the issues of " the complications of global religions" (175).

In "What Happened to Religion in Contemporary Art?" James Elkins writes how Slavoj Zizek described God as the ultimate tamagochi (a Japanese hand held game where you feed and entertain an imaginary pet). In this toy our compassion has been channelled into a private computer game about a God that puts demands upon us (176). Coincidentally Gupta has taken this further in the work "God.exe" (177). "God.exe" is a computer pop-up version of the Tamagochi toy.

I interacted with this work which gets to the crux of the issue. Is it real prayer or just a simulation of prayer that I made to the Tamagochi? I was led to experiment in my methods of prayer and perhaps the only answer to the question could come if there was an answer to the prayers that I made. There was not.

Other artists have experimented with different religious identities and faith in a secular, pluralistic context e.g. in his series of photographs "Life 1-4" 2003 the Tibetan artist Gonkar Gyatso depicted himself painting in different guises (with paintings and props appropriate to those guises) but in the same pose. His is a Buddhist monk, a Tibetan citizen, a secular artist, a Chinese Communist. This showed issues of shared identity and the elements within his own identity. And in "Disney plus-4" 2005 he even has a work where he made the image of the Buddha out of small images of Disney cartoon characters. However, whilst he is making links between parts of his identities Gupta was going further by asking the audience to make choices between identities and experimenting with new forms of worship.

Gupta's Postmodern Religious Artwork has the modernist form of commodity, irony and the secular, however, a semi-ironic space is made for a break through to non-commodifiable, sincere and sacred sentiments. This is constructive postmodernism as it may bring about utopian change out of a semi-ironic religious faith, rather than Modernist dialectics, spiritualism or scientific progress. However, there was not the mixing of different religious forms to characterise a truly postmodern position. Instead she was offering pre-modern options.

This pre-modern versus Modern tension was a conceptual block that would take the media some time to overcome. In 2004 a series of reality television shows also began, with the BBC program called "The Monastery" where five men spent 40 days in a monastery to see how it affected their lives. In 2005 "Spirituality Shopper" on Channel 4 was a program where people tried different religious perspectives to see how they coped. This treated religion as a commodity but was more sympathetic to the genuine change that might occur in participants' lives. However, it was still within the strict confines of traditional religious perspectives and methods of worship.

All of the above artists display some aspects of Postmodern Religious Art: the parasacred, multi-faith, multi-cultural use of popular media, kitsch, liminal bricolage, self-reinvention, performed acts (of meditation, preaching or worship), communal worship, anti-monopoly demonstration, political action. None of them have all these elements, but as postmodernism is non-essentialist they do not need to in order to be described as Postmodern Religious Artists.

Mark C. Taylor argued that both the transcendent art, of Modernism, and the immanent pop art, of a secular "postmodernism", were concerned with utopia. His view was that Modernism is characterised by utopian thinking and that radical division characterises postmodern thinking. I argue that the radical division is characterised by Modernist, mystical Gnosticism and that postmodern religion is non-extreme and does not assert single solutions. Rather, it is semi-ironic, about solutions.

Work that is spiritual or radical, or Anti-religious, or coming from Tantric, Buddhist and Gnostic mysticism is Modernist. Work that is anti-commodity is also Modernist as is work that is both reconstructive and pro-commodity. I suggest that Postmodern Religious Art is not essentialist, is semi-ironic and can include art that does not fit a strict set of characteristics.

The initial rejection of organised religion is replaced with individual and creative religion and the Modernist search for an essential synthesis is replaced with an individual, nominal expression.

Kant's aesthetic and spiritual dread and helplessness at the sublime in nature is then semi-overcome with a semi-ironic faith in the power of a religious commodity. Whether this semi-ironic faith can lead to any personal, physical or critical/political change is an experiment whose conclusion individuals need to decide for themselves.

The belief is primarily moral (like Dali's Surrealism A2) and the art-form is from these moral and narrative traditions (whether figurative or abstract B2) but is also involving a mystical breakdown of structure (like the Dadaists) that is secondary but always in the background, ensuring that the Prophetic artists never treats themselves as a God and that they reinvent themselves as part of a community of individuals who all have their valid beliefs. Consequently Postmodern Religious Art is a mixture of A2, B2 and B1, tempered by A1. It is also more conceptual and symbolic than it is expressive. The expression coming from religious devotion more than from a mystical aesthetic experience.

My own conclusion can be seen in relation to my own artwork.

MY OWN POSTMODERN RELIGIOUS ARTWORK

My art had become increasingly liminal and universal. Unconsciously I saw a need to become more specific and religious and so I began to include religious artefacts and elements of low culture in my work and to address issues of the conflict between religious and secular systems.

I developed "Club Religion" events in 2002, incorporating kitsch clubbing, with cultural forms of religion. This included music, lights, fashion, dancing, ritual and sculpture. "Club Religion" was a space where religious and secular faiths can come together in open-minded possibility, where energy was to be channelled into a positive moral effect and not just a hedonistic pleasure. My "scene" included an "Inter-religious Fancy Dress and Fashion Launch Party" at the Arts Café, London, 2002, accompanied with an exhibition of a series of mock fashion adverts for religion with the brand "Disco Art Religion".

In December 2002, New York, at Ground Zero, I created a DVD of my semi-ironic performance. I dressed as the prophet of Postmodern Religious Art, in clothes which I had bought on shopping sprees for objects from different religions. A red silk Catholic Bishops robe, rimmed with gold ribbon, a black Muslim hijab and yashmak on my face, a white Jewish prayer shawl, a Hindu temple banner rimmed in golden swastikas, a Hindu bag with a Sacred OM symbol on it, a rainbow coloured disco ball necklace and finally a halo, a pair of disco boppers.

I had bought a black plastic baby doll, which I adorned with a halo of disco boppers and Israeli flag nappies. I then began to paint a Rainbow Swastika on her, whilst kneeling in the snow. My fingers froze as I painted.

By creating my own semi-ironic Messiah, Eve II, I symbolised the negative and destructive energies at Ground Zero into a new narrative with Eve II I returned an Apple (symbolising New York – the Big Apple) to a nearby tree (the Biblical Tree of knowledge of good and evil) and turned it into a Biblical Tree of Life (world economic aid). This new Eden is opposed to the tree of death that invading Eden (associated with Mesopotamia and Iraq) generated.

With Eve II I symbolically join the Judaeo Christian narrative tradition of a masculine Messiah with the feminine Eastern mystical tradition by way of the rainbow swastika painted on her chest (not the Nazi war symbol but a Hindu symbol of peace and good luck).

I commemorated the plastic doll of Eve II (and plastic ideals she stood for) in a painting "The Eve II Revelation", 2003. This follows in the tradition of Kaspar David Friedrich but was a vision of the prophet Elijah riding out of the sky on a golden chariot she flies out at the spectator, with 7 religious figures beneath her (the highest one being the prophet of Postmodern Religious Art).

I posed, for photographic studies for the painting, on top of a freezing mountain, Great Gable in the Lake District (the birth place of English Romanticism). On the final pose, (costume/identity 7, where I was naked,) out of the clouds, in exactly the place where Eve II would appear, a rescue helicopter appeared. Symbolically I represented how Eve II, a parasacred Messiah, breaks through the abstractions of Modernism to give a revelation of how we can now choose from a range of religious options and combinations. In my painting "The Eve II Revelation" the figure breaks out of liminality and expresses Messianicity. It nods to Modernist non-duality for its origin but calls for moral action by questioning cultural and religious dogmatism.

Eve II was given the role of founder of "Divinityland". An art series where I mixed together kitsch religious buildings and where figures of Jesus and Krishna race on cars. This was a series of play-sets, performances and installations (including a theme-park made of giant cardboard cut-out religious toys at Liverpool Biennial 2004). My racing Jesus against Krishna as racing stars and depicting Jesus or Buddhas as star footballers presented religious figures as secular heroes and made a reverse move of showing how religious high culture can be transformed into cultural forms. My educational workshops also featured in the Daily Mail, the Times and BBC Radio 4, causing controversy and raising positive debate before the

Danish Cartoon created a complete polarisation of the sacred and the secular.

However, I was soon to lose even the least ironic of my religious faith. None of the art galleries weren't open to experimental art about God and religion. Every time I submitted work to the curators would turn me down and refuse to give any reasons. But religion was and still is the most important issue in the world and the nation's public galleries should show art addressing it.

I didn't care about the money. I was a religious artist. I made art because I wanted to express the truth in an aesthetic way and wanted to share this. However, to communicate to the galleries my solution was to make art that would teach them the benefits of religion in business. I did this as a "Business Messiah" that incorporates religion into business structures, showing them how to increase market share by moving towards religious management models and religious products. So in 2005 I submitted a proposal to Tate Modern to create a performance about Religion, democracy, consumer globalisation and fundamentalism around a reconstruction, made of sugar cubes, of Sir Henry Tate's Memorial. As the original Tate gallery was created by Sir Henry Tate (an active Unitarian) and Unitarianism influenced the US constitution and provided the prime model of consumer "pick n mix" religious democracy this was timely and original.

Unitarianism grew in the 17th century out of Christianity and was of particular interest as it rejects any form of discrimination and promotes all to become ministers regardless of gender, sexual orientation, race and also promotes same sex marriage. Unitarianism also allows people of other religions, e.g. Muslim or Jewish Unitarian, to be members. Unitarianism gives a meta-view, i.e. concerns beliefs about the way we believe in freedom, rationality, respect, openness, diversity, and this has united Unitarians, since the 19th century, in their search for religious, artistic or scientific truths. Unitarians can have any belief – even atheistic or Trinitarian – as the important element is common unity through respecting the rights of individuals.

When I was rejected without reasons I began a case of discrimination within the Employment Equality (Religion of Belief) Regulations 2003 at the Employment Tribunals, claiming that Sir Nicholas Serota, the Director of the Tate Gallery, was guilty of religious discrimination against me for not selecting my performance for their performance programme. I argued that the gallery only showed art that was spiritual or was offensive to Christians. I also argued that the Prime Minister, Mr Tony Blair, was responsible for employing the Director so was also guilty of discrimination.

The statistics (all that was needed as proof in a Tribunal case) showed that the works presented at the Tate were atheistic, expressed some kind of vague mysticism or were directly offensive towards Christianity. "Religious" art was not included and this clearly implied that the curators were discriminatory against religious artists and their art. Rejection of anything concerning religion was endemic in the art-world and the curators were thus following indirect discriminatory practice.

A number of assumptions were made concerning the nature of art and religion when curators made decisions. The Tate, educational establishments, international art fairs (largely commercial) and state funded art programs all take many of their cues from commercial galleries, where discrimination is present.

The Tate is part of a contemporary art-world that has a religious/belief bias that is largely based in "critical thinking", atheism, spiritualism, pantheism, the "everyday", liminality, scatological Gnosticism and quasi-socialism. the content that is allowed in contemporary art is also largely atheistic, Modernist, spiritual or ironically/negatively religious.

It is a fallacy to think that you cannot regulate the selection of art as (despite claims that the appreciation of art is all subjective and that "Beauty is in the eye of the beholder") there is a consensus amongst scholars about the principles of classical art - based on originality, draughtsmanship, composition, form, tone, perspective, brush-stroke, colour, light, narrative, meaning, etc. And even though Modern art is about ideas as well as beauty, it kept many of these standards and can still be systematised. But rich collectors don't want a system. They want to be free to pick and choose art on a whim. What was and still is needed are regulations for how art is selected to ensure fairness, otherwise the selectors are unaccountable.

It is also a fallacy to think that regulations would just destroy creativity as regulation would ensure maximum creativity occurs, because it would stop the same old ideas and styles of work from being repeated and passed off as original and would mean that the creative contribution of all kinds of people would be valued. But racist, sexist, anti-religious art continues to flourish because the art world is controlled by the collectors, many of whom are bankers and from corporations who are against regulations.

Tate takes its cues from the worlds of commercial art, state art and the mainstream media – all of which currently operate levels of religious discrimination. This institutional discrimination is like institutional racism, only against religious believers. It is the job of the Tate Curators, Director and Trustees, as guardians of the public interest, to determine what is of significance and relevance in contemporary art in Britain and internationally. This means that they should ensure that the art business does not operate solely for financial ends and that public galleries implement correct policy.

Their selection isn't just artistic preference, it's bias, and it's been getting worse with the violent work of artists like Damien Hirst. He mocks religion, with his pretend Satanism, slicing cows in half as sacrifices to the God of money. The works are evil. But you aren't allowed to say this to the liberal art-world. They say his art makes us look at the world with fresh eyes. But society is just being manipulated and infected with Hirst's "values". The galleries are socially engineering people into being anti-religious and censoring any real protest because they are dictated to by corporate collectors who only want art that celebrates brutal, selfish capitalism. Religion is banned.

It is claimed that the best art has always been commissioned by the rich. And that's the problem. The system of the rich selecting art hasn't changed since the times of the Medici family in Renaissance Italy. And the Medicis were worse than the Mafia. They murdered and cheated their way to the top and even put their own corrupt Pope into power.

Similarly, the art world is run by oil corporations and financial institutions who use art as a way to culturally dominate us. It's the same as the way that Adolf Hitler used art as propaganda. He exhibited classical German Art to promote Aryan purity and only put on exhibitions of Modern art to show that it was the "degenerate" art of Jewish profiteers. These were his unregulated, "subjective" choices. Regulations would have prevented the Nazis from selling art-works (by Braque, Chagall, Gauguin, Van Gogh, Picasso etc), stolen from Holocaust victims, to US collectors at the Galerie Fischer in Lucerne, Switzerland. But there were no such regulations because many of these collectors were linked to companies that had business dealings with the Nazis.

The works are now in the collections of patrons like the Rothschilds' The Bank of Manhattan and corporate sponsors, like British Petroleum and the Union Bank of Switzerland (UBS). The Tate displays these works and this both enhances the sponsor's corporate image and boosts the value of the art and buyers bid for their own works from their own auction houses to artificially inflate their prices.

The recent Chairmen of the Sugar Trustees have all worked for the Rothschild banks, and the Rothschilds recently worked with the Prime Minister to raise funds to purchase US art for the Tate. And when the Prime Minister lefts office his new job was with a subsidiary of the Rothschilds' Bank.

Corporations use art sponsorship for financial gain and also for cultural domination. Tate put on an exhibition "The Real Thing: Contemporary Art from China" and shortly after this the China Investment Corp put a $3 billion, 10% stake, into a Rothschild Private Equity group. At that point the Rothschilds donated £5 million to the Tate. The exhibition was a sweetener to get the Chinese to do a deal with the Rothschilds but it was also a part of a plan to change Chinese culture, by encouraging Chinese artists to join the corporate collectors in their Satanic program, of celebrating sex, money and violence. Chinese artists now made photographs of

Gods worshipping mobile phones, Christ crucified on cans of coke, and Christ with his genitals hanging out.

The Chinese, the Saudis and the Asian countries have financial reserves earned from manufacturing and oil sales and the Western financial firms opened these reserves up, getting the countries to invest in their Private Equity firms that sell high risk loans whose values are artificially hiked because they are based on projected returns. They're just like the artificially high art prices. And just like the art market, the value of these companies was based on a house of cards. So when it collapsed these countries lost heavily. This whole agenda was corrupt.

My case was rejected after two years legal battle and my website was closed down by Tate (despite their collection containing works by Hans Haacke an artist who made art works that were legal cases and the exposing of gallery corruption). My claim was "perversely" rejected on the grounds that my application was for the provision of goods rather than for a performance of work. So the issues of discrimination never got to be heard.

The Court of Appeal upheld this rejection and I was threatened again with a £50,000 legal bill from the Tate. Almost no press reported on the case, despite my also having a major exhibition about the case (including a version of the sugar cube memorial) next door to Tate Liverpool when they held the Turner Prize in 2007.

Throughout the case I had made art works of how I prayed for help from God, and in 2005/6 I even went on pilgrimage to holy sites in Jerusalem to film praying for help at different holy sites. The case had failed. My faith in Postmodern Religious Art was now completely broken.

MY INFLUENCE ON RECENT ARTISTS

My Tribunal case was seminal and defined the limit of what Postmodern Religious Art can be. In order to be consistent with a semi-ironic faith I was not prepared to risk complete financial ruin. Self-sacrifice and mortification is a characteristic of Modernist

Gnostic breakdown of religion or of Pre-modern sacrifice or self or others in a non-ironic religious ideology.

I brought about some important changes. The Tate Gallery announced that it was addressing the discriminatory balance of the work in its collection. However, the Tate made discrimination issues into those of sexual discrimination and a review was presented to the media by Tracey Emin. This exposed the difference in the way male and female artists were paid, e.g. how Damien Hirst's "Hymn" 1996 (a large sculptural copy of a small anatomical model) sold for £1 million whereas Tracy Emin's iconic "My Bed" 1999 (a constructed version of her own unmade bed) sold for £150,000. Artists such as Barbara Hepworth, Frida Kahlo, Bridget Riley, Rebecca Horn, Louise Bourgeois, Cindy Sherman and Gillian Wearing were shown by Tate but only 12% of the Tate Galleries' collection were by women artists. However, this review it did not address issues of religious discrimination.

Instead, they quietly began to show more religious art but it had to be by young Muslims, Hindus or Sikh, e.g. like Yara el-Sherbini 's video art "A Demonstration" 2005, a DIY instruction on how to make a bomb using a football, an empty toilet roll. She has various examples of bombs that she made earlier such as "A Carpet Bomb" 2005 which is in a Persian carpet rug. The work is a parody, a dark social satire with political commentary about what we watch and learn when it comes to how Muslims are represented in the Media. Or like Shadi Ghadirian's "Untitled" 2008 from the "Like Everday Series" has a person in a patterned headdress and veil but holding their hand in front of their face. The person wears a washing up glove and this humorously conveys a message of the oppression of women, not just from the veil but also from domestic chores. This is all a way to make Muslims feel included in the "art game." So the art-world can sell art to rich Saudis whilst maintaining a climate that makes fun of religion.

After my case a number of artists from ethnic backgrounds who I had influenced in my work (e.g. Shezad Dawood and Harminder Singh) made artworks about their religions and were accepted by the Tate. They were just making random works that mixed up art and religious forms in a way that was a breakdown of structure.

Shezad Dawood is an artist that I influenced who saw my Inter-religious art work in the Arts Café, London in 2002. He has looked at the commodification of religion and created performance art pieces where he painted himself blue like Krishna or other Hindu deities whilst performing everyday and secular activities. This breaks down the high status of the religious figures, e.g. "Feature" 2008. However, without a clear religious direction this work falls back into the position of a liminal breakdown that has Gnostic, mystical implications (rather than religious ones). This work was exhibiterd as part of the Tate Triennial 2009 where the theme was a new art tern proposed by Nicolas Bourriaud, the Altermodern. This is supposed to be the period after postmodernism where a globalised culture has been created through increased communication, travel and migration.

Now any work about anything is acceptable and the way of selecting is a process completely shrouded in unclear curatorial terms like the "Altermodern". It is a mix of commercial and public. Where the public galleries are like private sector galleries whose board members are from large corporations. Who commissions the work is key to contemporary art. The only regulator is money. This Altermodern Globalisation is really just the shifting of financial control in art.

Thus the Chinese, Indians, Brazilians and Russians (the emerging economies) along with the Middle East Oil states will dictate what is art. At the moment the artists from these countries are creating anti-religious or spiritual work so that they can fit in with the art system. However as these countries (which comprise of practicing Confucians, Daoists, Buddhists, Hindus, Christians and Muslims) gain more power over Western economies then you will inevitably get more Postmodern Religious Art. They will find themselves in positions of economic superiority and will make work that directly expresses their religious beliefs.

Harminder Singh Judge is an artist that I also influenced who e-mailed me about my "Religion Cabaret with Divinityland and Rainbow Swastika Alien Encounter" at Edinburgh Fringe in 2005. He is a performance and installation artist who uses ritual, dress, sound, prayer, food and protocol to construct a new sensory and religious language. He is a Sikh who combines this with Hindu myth and secular culture. He investigates how cultures represent the divine and how symbols travel between different cultures.

Harminder, however, has been influenced into the Gnostic ideology of the secular figures who use atavistic religious forces and see performance artists as needing to become Gnostic sacrifices. He has been mentored by Franco B in the London Performance Art scene. As such it moves away from Postmodern Religious Art to deconstructive Modernist Gnosticism.

"The Modes of Al-Ikseer" 2009-10, was a performance installation incorporating live music and based on an epic Hindu tale called the Churning of the Ocean and on the artist's love of 1980's electro pop music, namely Depeche Mode's "Personal Jesus" (later covered by Marilyn Manson).

The artist was dressed in traditional Hindu costume and wore a neon sculpture that read 'Pick up the receiver, I'll make you a believer' as he rotates upon a shallow pool containing up to 2,500 litres of 'milk' upon an aluminium platform with in-built LED lighting whilst a soundtrack of mythic animal noises and distorted guitars and synthesizers is played. In his feat of endurance a reference is made to the pop world's hedonism, but there is a double irony as the artist forces the viewer back from Depeche Mode's rejection of faith to a statement of positive acceptance of religion – yet within a sexually charged and commodified art environment.

These artists used religious personas or religious images in a semi-ironic way, unsure of their identity. But they were too late as the whole Postmodern Religious Art process that I had begun was finished and no longer had any authenticity. There was no justice, truth, fairness or Divine intervention in the art system. Such justice and fairness is a hallmark of religion and as religious artists they had done nothing to ensure that my work was fairly treated and seen as an influence on them. This also reflected on the hollow corruption of that commodity system.

Other works that presented a challenge to the gallery or religious systems include Terry Hammill's application to the Vatican for a Sainthood, claiming that his miracle was to turn base materials into artworks. The application was rejected but his claim had been made in semi-ironic faith of success. It was an avenue for genuine engagement with the religious world to cross over between faith and art. Hammill's art practice includes an abortive moon mission and an attempt to stage an opera in the Australian desert. They are humorous failures to achieve unrealisable goals.

Another work is Patrick Braxton-Hicks' 2007 image of Jesus with Osama Bin Laden's face and Vera Pelle's Virgin Mary in a Burkha/Yashmak. This shows the link between early Christianity and Islam. It is an exploration of religious links but is academic as it is not a clear expression of personal faith.

A more progressive, lifestyle option was presented by Architect, Nigel Coates designed the "Batterseum" 2009 to turn the abandoned Batttersea Power Station, London into a park themed on religion, with mosque-like, church-like and temple like structures around the park to allude to worship, rather than be the setting for organised religious services.

POST-POSTMODERN RELIGIOUS ART

The blocking of my Tribunal case destroyed my belief in Postmodern Religious Art. My reaction was to pray. I had turned away from art and wanted to turn to religious truth. I realised that I had been influenced by the Devil in the art I had produced and that the most religious of works was text, the written work, e.g. the Torah, the Koran, The Bhagavad Gita, the Guru Granth Sahib, the Bible. This returned art back into being a tool of religion and, in 2007-9, I put down my experiences, ideas and prophecies in a book "The Rainbow Swastika Conspiracy" (178). This is a story to preserve and pass on my original ideas and it was also to try and create a work of genuine faith.

The book describes both a "Register Of Originality" (for controlling the selection of art in the artworld in order to make it fair and just) and also an organisation called "The Auditors Of God", a religious body that has a "Register Of Religious Businesses" to create a Fair Trade type system that prevents religious believers using corrupt companies or banks involved in usury. This organisation is a pre-modern use of technology, and is an antidote to Modernism and its Simulation that is postmodernism.

I am making a Wiki website for both of these. A Wiki is a website that anyone can contribute to in order for it to grow and develop. I am working on creating these as the only way forward for art. These may work until businesses and art organisations block the site, as it will lose them money or make them accountable for their decisions.

The book also dramatised some prophecies about the art and business worlds. This gave a more religious dimension to my work. I was inspired, perhaps Divinely, to write about the corrupt art Elite, who are driven by a desire to destroy the world. This is a death drive of Freud, and activates when people are in states of anger as they see the destruction of things around them as something pure and cleansing. They believe there is something beyond the world, a mystical dimension, but because they are so caught up in the world the only way that they can unconsciously think to reach the mystical world is to destroy the real world.

So I described that whilst the liberal Elite claim to follow a spiritual line of thought that unites all belief systems, this really just hides their prejudices and greed. And I dramatise this unconscious drive as if it is conscious drive to destroy our climate and the planet. It is part of an economic war between the US and China that is manipulated, behind the scenes, by a global banking Elite.

The Elite worship Zurvan, the God of infinite time, whose children were Ahura Mazda and Ahriman the Gods of Good and Evil, Light and Dark. The Jews made Ahura Mazda supreme and called him Jehovah, who the Gnostic Elite call the Demi-urge, the jealous God who trapped humans' souls in his prison world and stopped us from returning to Zurvan. But beneath Jehovah, in Persian influenced sections of the Old Testament, were the 7 angels. One of whom was Mithras, Lucifer, the bringer of Inner Light. In the Bible he is one of God's angels, a Seraph, a fiery serpent, who opened the eyes of Adam and Eve, for which the Demi-urge expelled him from Heaven.

The Elite follow the Qabbalistic numerology that teaches that the value of the Serpent and of the Messiah, are both 358. That Mithras/Lucifer and the Demiurge/Jehovah are one and the same being. The Elite work to evolve the earth towards a final unity of darkness and light in the Oneness of Zurvan, through Mithras the Angel of Wisdom.

And now, for the Elite to bring about the New Age the Demi-urge must unite with Satan. This is why the final Christ will be the Anti-Christ. The Earth Mother will unite with the Sky God, in a war to end wars. This final Messiah will be a warrior and these teachings of the Aryan Masters were passed down through history, by the Mithraists, the Gnostics, the Knights Templar, the Kabbalists, the Freemasons. Passed down by warriors who preserved the secret teachings of Mithras, that brutality is needed to bring about change.

This is how I propose that the Freudian death drive perspective employed by the Modern Art world relates to world religions. My prophecies were fictional dramatisations but elements of truth are contained in them. Whilst the beliefs may not be conscious there are cultural resonances present and operating unconsciously. And these resonances are still having terrible effects on the world. If is for religious believes to engage in debate with the art-world and to oppose this direction.

I am from the Prophetic Jewish tradition and am completely against the Mystical Aryan tradition. It is for all of us to try and prevent this. To waken the Elite and ourselves from their unconscious sleep in the world of the Simulacrum before we all to destroy ourselves and the real world.

POSTMODERN ART CONCLUSION

In order to conclude about Postmodern Religious Art we need to look at the full story of religious art. The story began with Animism, which was a mixture of beliefs and art forms. According to our scheme the following combinations of art and belief forms developed.

A1 – the mystical was expressed in abstract art, e.g. Hindu Mandalas. In its modern form this connected to natural forces and was part of an exploration of art as well as an expression of dry mysticism) but ended in a dry academic exploration, e.g. Modern abstract art, Romanticism and Abstract expressionism. The radical breakdown of structure of the Dadaists and of Anton Artaud can also be included in this category.

A2 – the moral was wholly or mainly represented in figurative art, e.g. Greek Polytheism, Dali's Surrealism, Social Realism, Warhol's Pop Art, the art of the YBAs and Gomez Pena. This kind of art was for religious, fascist, commercial or revolutionary moral (or immoral) ends.

B1 – the mystical was indirectly expressed in figurative art. This was to convey complex ideas to a mass audience, e.g. Hindu and Buddhist statues, or to give art objects a sense of mystical mystery, e.g. in the Modern work of Joseph Beuys, Bill Viola and Anthony Gormley, or as a process of breaking down figures moving from B! to A1, e.g. Dadaism and Anton Artaud.

B2 – the moral indirectly represented with a symbolism of ideas of the Divine, e.g. Jewish and Islamic design, or as part of a symbolic system that conveyed moral notions but wasn't clearly figurative, e.g. Thomas Hirschhorn, or dry academic art, e.g. Dan Flavin and art about the nature of art.

In contrast to the above Postmodern Religious Art is a mixture of art forms, as diverse and searching for meaning as that of the original Animists (separated by tribe and nation). Their quest for truth has now been appropriated by dominant, ruling powers into systems of control and government. The only way to counter this dominance is to require regulation for this art and government.

Before continuing our conclusion we will look at the different categories of Modern art that we have been considering (expressive, analytic and symbolic) as these also relate to our schema and throw light upon it.

Expressive – this is the wild energy given a form and an ordered structure, e.g. via abstract expressionism or performance. Creating art combines expression with a degree of analysis and methodology but this puts expression as primary. Ultimately mystical expression is suited to abstraction A1 and emotional expression to narrative A2.

Analytic – this is the content and meaning whether a figure or a narrative scene. This can occur in A1, A2, B1 or B2 but is more suited to A2.

Symbolic – this is using one thing to show another thing or concept. As such the relationship is indirect and best suited to the way that abstract can show a figure B2 or a figure can show abstract ideas B1.

The conclusion remains the same. The diverse expressions of art and religion are a way to address the issue of whether the mystical and the moral are primary.

There is no definite answer either way, it is just a question of choice or instinct to prefer one or the other. Art expresses a variety of these positions and also balances psychological excesses as they arise in society.

Mysticism is too abstract for most people and if made the dominant cultural force it is hijacked by the corrupt Elite who do not understand it. They use it to confuse the general population so that they can be pacified and exploited with material products.

Morality is more open to mass understanding but means that the general populace can judge the Elite, which they do not want, so they use economic systems to prevent regulations and judgments being put in place. Art without regulation is used as a mechanism of control by the Elite. Society has now reached a point where most forms of expression have been made and a clear system of art regulation can be put into place. This will increase fairness and understanding in society and undermine exploitation of the general populace by the Elite. Religion also serves as a mechanism of regulation of the Elite but also results in its own religious Elite.

So, there was no certainty in Animism and nor is there any certainty in Postmodern Religious Art. Uniquely, because of this both movements are nearest to the Divine truth and nearest to a psychologically balanced artistic expression.

The many edifices of religion, e.g. Islam, or of secular atheism were all created to give metaphysical certainty and control. If one of these edifices becomes dominant then the others need to oppose it – because the greatest truth is that none of them can be known for certain.

In all of this we find that art is secondary and expressive of a religion (rather than formative of religion) or balances the religion with its opposite art form. Even in Modernity art is secondary as Modern society has found its balance by using postmodern art.

Benjamin Constant said that "Art for art's sake, with no purpose, for any purpose perverts art. But art achieves a purpose which is not its own." This is not correct as this purely aesthetic art only arises from a technologically driven Modern society. Such art, free of content, would not arise if it were not for the surplus of consumer content that we produce in ordinary life. As such the more meaning we create outside of the galleries the less we will need inside the galleries. As the Modernist architect Frank Lloyd Wright said "Art for art's sake is a philosophy of the well fed."

Those that do not have this surplus of consumer content reject this system with art that has an opposing content of its own. So the more equality we have in a Modern world then the less need there will be for Postmodern Religious Art. However, as the Elite are morally flawed this need continues. So the rise in production of Modern Art can be symptomatic of either the Elite's corruption or of an increase in social equality (as everyone is gaining access to the trappings of Elitism). However the rise of Pre-modern Religious Art and Postmodern Religious Art can only be symptomatic of a broader social inequality and a rebellion against this Elite.

REFERENCES

(1) Mookerjee, Priya. Pathway Icons: The Wayside Art of India. Thames & Hudson 1987 pp4-8
(2) Kessler, Herbert L. Spiritual Seeing, University of Pennsylvania Press 2000 p1-3
(3) Elkins, James "What Happened to Religion in Contemporary Art?"
http://www.jameselkins.com/Texts/a/religion.html, 2004 pp6-8
(4) Taylor, Mark C. Disfiguring, Univ. of Chicago Press, 1992 pp21-33
(5) Taylor, Mark C. Op.cit, pp34-45
(6) Koerner, Joseph Leo. Caspar David Friedrich and the subject of landscape. Reaktion 1990 p164
(7) Koerner, Op. cit. p217
(8) Koerner, Op. cit. p15
(9) Edwards, Cliff. Van Gogh and God: A Creative Spiritual Quest. Loyola University Press, 1989. p. 115. ISBN 0-8294-0621-2
(10) Taylor, Mark C. Op.cit, p54
(11) Golding, John. Paths to the Absolute: Mondrian, Malevich, Kandinsky, Pollock, Newman, Rothko and Still, Thames & Hudson, 2000, p14
(12) Golding, Op. cit. p157
(13) Ward, Glen. Postmodernism, Hodder Headline Limited, 2003 pp78-80
(14) Golding, Op. cit. p74
(15) Golding, Op. cit. p78
(16) Golding, Op. cit. p110.
(17) Golding, Op. cit. p107
(18) Bohm-Duchen, Monica. Chagall Phaidon 1998 p133
(19) Bohm-Duchen, Op. cit. p133
(20) Greenberg, Clement. Avant-Garde and Kitsch 1939, in Art in Theory 1900-1990 Harrison, Charles and Wood, Paul (Eds) Blackwell 1998 p534
(21) Greenberg, Op. cit. p539
(22) Greenberg, Op. cit. pp774-5
(23) Newman, Michael. Revising Modernism, Representing Postmodernism, in "Postmodernism: ICA documents" 1985 p 103
(24) Ward, Glen. Op.cit, p81
(25) Benjamin, Walter. "Dream City and Dream House, Dreams of the Future, Anthropological Nihilism, Jung" The Arcades Project trans. Howard Eiland and Kevin McLaughlin, London and Cambridge, Ma: Harvard University Press 1999, K2,3, p527
(26) Buck-Morss, Susan, "Dream World of Mass Culture", The Dialectics of Seeing: Walter Benjamin and the Arcades Project MIT Press 1991, p268
(27) Benjamin, Walter, Op.cit, pp391-2
(28) Adorno, Theodor and Horkheimer, Max."The Culture Industry", Adorno, Theodor The Culture Industry: Selected Essays on Mass Culture Rouledge 1999, pp38-41
(29) Bradley, Fiona. Gala Dali : The Eternal Feminine in Salvador Dali: A Mythology Tate 1998, p68
(30) Gibson, Ian The Shameful Life of Salvador Dali Faber and Faber 1997, pp506-7
(31) Bradley, Op. cit. p24
(32) Golding, Op. cit. p194
(33) Golding, Op. cit. p116
(34) Golding, Op. cit. p126

162

(35) Golding, Op. cit. pp133-4
(36) Golding, Op. cit. p137
(37) Golding, Op. cit. p201
(38) Katerina Clark and Michael Holquist, Chapter 14 – Rabelais and His World, in *Mikhael Bakhtin*, Harvard College, 1984, pp. 295-320
(39) Bois, Yve-Alain. "The Use Value of "Formless"", in Bois, Yve-Alain and Rosalind Krauss, *Formless: A User's Guide*, New York (Zone Books), 1997, pp.26
(40) Bois, Op. cit. p 17
(41) Bois, Op. cit. p30
(42) Bois, Op. cit. p37
(43) Bois, Op. cit. p32
(44) Artaud, Antonin, "Two Letters on Cruelty" in *The Theater and its Double*, trans Corti, Victor, Calder Publications, 1999
(45) Artaud, Antonin, "Seraphim's Theatre" in *The Theater and its Double*, trans Corti, Victor, Calder Publications, 1999 p101
(46) Artaud, Antonin, "An Affective Athleticism" in *The Theater and its Double*, trans Corti, Victor, Calder Publications, 1999 p92
(47) Goodall, Jane *Artaud and the Gnostic Drama* Clarendon Press Oxford 1994 p215
(48) Goodall, Op. Cit. p208
(49) Goodall, Op. Cit. p4
(50) Goodall, Op. Cit. p217
(51) Artaud, Antonin, "Seraphim's Theatre" Op. Cit. p101
(52) Baker-White, Op. Cit p203
(53) Benjamin H.D. Buchloh: 'Beuys: The Twilight of the Idol,' Artforum, vol.5, no.18, pp.35-43
54) Tappe, Anselm, *Guy Debord*, Univ. of California Press, 1999, p34
55) Tappe, Op.cit, p40
56) Buck-Morss, Op.cit, p268
57) Buck-Morss, Op.cit, p260
58) Benjamin, Op.cit, p391-2
(59) Sayre, Henry. M. *The Object of Performance : the American avant-garde since 1970*. University of Chicago Press 1992, p6
(60) Newman, Op. cit. p105
(61) Chris Burden in Fineberg, Jonathan, "Art Since 1940: Strategies of Being" Englewood Cliffs: Prentice Hall, 1995, p342
(62) Goldberg, RoseLee *Performance: Live Art since the 60's* Thames and Hudson 1998
(63) Sayre, Op. cit. p13
(64) Freeland, Cynthia. Art Theory: A Very Short Introduction, Oxford University Press, 2003. pp44-46
(65) Freeland, Op.cit, p49
(66) Ward, Op cit, pp169-173
(67) Sayre, Op.cit, p31
(68) Newman, Op. cit. p127
(69) http://www.guggenheim.org/exhibitions/warhol/warhol_bottom_index.html
(70) Ward, Op.cit, pp63-76
(71) Newman, Op. cit. p136
(72) Taylor, Op.cit, p317
(73) Ward, Op.cit, p170
(74) Ward, Op.cit, pp95-97

(75) Ward, Op.cit, p105
(76) Ward, Op.cit, p106
(77) Derrida, Jacques Chapter 1 "Faith and Knowledge: The Two Sources of "Religion" at the Limits of Reason Alone" 1996 Acts of Religion. New York: Routledge, 2002. p55
(78) Taylor, Op.cit, p266
(79) Goodall, Op. Cit. p208
(80) Ward, Op.cit, p99-100
(81) Taylor, Op.cit, pp233 Bataille, Georges. Theory of Religion (trans. Robert Hurley (New York: Zone Books, 1989))
(82) Taylor, p236 Bataille, Georges Op.cit,
(83) Taylor, Op.cit, p267
(84) Taylor, Op.cit, pp233-240
(85) Goodall, Jane. Artaud and the Gnostic Drama Clarendon Press Oxford, 1994 p217
(86) Goodall, Op. Cit. p217
(87) Goodall, Op. Cit. p17
(88) Broadhurst, Susan Liminal Acts: A Critical Overview of Contemporary Performance and Theory Cassell 2000 p34
(89) Baas, Jacquelyn and Jacob, Mary Jane. "Buddha Mind In Contemporary Art", University of California Press, 2004 p 240 - 247
(90) Cecil, Paul. Even Further: The Metaphysics of Sigils in "Painful but Fabulous: The Lives and Art of Genesis P-Orridge" Soft Skull Press 2002 p122
(91) Jackson, Kevin. Talk of the Town, "Independent on Sunday", 1 June 2003
(92) Wilson, Julie. As It Is in "Painful but Fabulous: The Lives and Art of Genesis P-Orridge" Soft Skull Press 2002 p85
(93) Enwezor, Okuwi, "The Black Box", Documenta XI exhibition catalogue (2002), p47
(94) Levin, Kim. "More Is More" Village Voice, November 27, 2002, p64
(95) Stallabrass, Julian. High Art Lite, Verso 1999, p286
(96)Tate Magazine, Issue 3, http://www.tate.org.uk/magazine/issue3/michaellandy.htm
(97) Stallabrass, Op.cit, p75-9
(98) Stallabrass, Op.cit, p75-9
(99) Fiat, Christopher. "The Experience of Violence in Sacrifice", Documenta XI exhibition catalogue (2002)
(100) Stallabrass, Op.cit, p241
(101) Stallabrass, Op.cit, p253
(102) Roberts, John. "Domestic Squabble" in Who's Afraid of Red, White and Blue? Burrows, David (ed), University of Central England, Birmingham, Article Press, 1998, p46
(103) Roberts, Op cit, p50
(104) Stallabrass, Op.cit, p123
(105) Quinn, Malcolm "The Legions of the Blind: the Philistine and Cultural Studies", Beech and Roberts (eds.) The Philistine Controversy Verso 2002. p271.
(106) Enwezor, Op.cit, p43.
(107) Enwezor, Op.cit, p48
(108) http://www.palestinefacts.org/pf_early_palestine_name_origin.php
(109) Stallabras, Op.cit, p3
(110) Stallabras, Op.cit, p139

(111) Stallabraas, Op.cit. p271
(112) Stallabras, Op.cit. p123
(113) Stallabras, Op.cit. p99
(114) Stallabras, Op.cit. p230
(115) Stallabras, Op.cit. p232
(116) Stallabras, Op.cit. p230
(117) Stallabras, Op.cit. p280
(118) John Roberts, "Domestic Squabbles", in *Who's Afraid of Red, White and Blue?*, p50
(119) Stallabras, Op.cit. p210
(120) Stallabras, Op.cit. p274
(121) Stallabras, Op.cit. p153
(122) Douglas Foght, London, February 27, 1995 LAAT
www.vpro.nl/data/laat/materiaal/chapman-bros-interview.shtml
(123) Maia Damianovic, *Journal of Contemporary Art* 1997 www.jca-online.com
(124) Mark Sladen, "The Body in Question", *Art Monthly*, no 191, 1995
(125) Dinos Chapman, "Gender is an Organic Superstition", *MAKE: The Magazine of Womens' Art*, Aug/Sept 1996, p18-9
(126) David Falconer, "Doctorin' the Retardis" in *Chapmanworld*
(127) Falconer, ibid
(128) Falconer, ibid
(129) Falconer, ibid
(130) Douglas Fogle, "A Scatological Aesthetics for the Tired of Seeing" in *Chapmanworld*,
(131) Fogle, ibid
(132) Martha Schwendener, "Gagosian", *New Art Examiner*, vol 25, Dec 97/Jan 98, p46
(133) Schwendener, ibid p46
(134) Rosenblum, Chapman and Chapman, ibid p
(135) Whitehead, Jayson. *The Reverend Billy Wants You to Stop Shopping* in "Oldspeak", the Rutherford Institute's Journal,
http://www.rutherford.org/articles/oldspeak-revbilly.asp
(136) Whitehead, op. cit.
137) Ward, Op.cit, pp84-85
138) Ward, Op.cit, p124 referencing Poster, Mark "Postmodern Virtualities" in Futurenatural 1996
139) Ward, Op.cit, p124
(140) Baas, Jacquelyn and Jacob, Mary Jane. Op.cit. p 258 - 263
(141) Fox, Matthew, A Mystical Cosmology: Toward a Postmodern Spirituality in Ray Griffin, David (Ed). "Sacred Interconnections: Postmodern Spirituality, Political Economy, and Art" p30
(142) Flamiano, Dominic. "A Conversation with Jill Martin" leaflet by Techno Cosmic Mass – undated c. 2000
(143) Tucker, Jill *Rave Spirituality* in "The Oakland Tribune" (undated)
(144) http://www.technocosmicmass.org/pages/about_friends/about_friends.html
(145) Enwezor, Op.cit, p47-48
(146) Woodhead, Linda and Heelas, Paul (ed). *Religion in Modern Times*, Blackwell 2000 p 477
(147) Pavis, Patrice. "Introduction: Towards a Theory of Interculturalism in Theatre?" Pavis, Patrice. (Ed) *The Intercultural Performance Reader*. Routledge 1996 pp4-17

(148) Doss, Erika. *Twentieth-Century American Art,* Oxford, 2002
(149) Gomez Pena, Guillermo. *Dangerous Border Crossers: the artist talks back* Routledge 2000 p240
(150) Gomez Pena, Op.cit. pp236-7
(151) Gomez Pena, Op.cit. p242
(152) Gomez-Pena, Guillermo & Sifuentes, Roberto. Temple of Confessions: Mexican Beasts and Living Santos, Powerhouse Books 1996 p10
(153) Gomez-Pena & Sifuentes, Op. cit. p21
(154) Gomez-Pena & Sifuentes, Op. cit. p19
(155) Gomez-Pena & Sifuentes, Op. cit. p22
(156) Gomez-Pena, Op.cit. p179
(157) Gomez-Pena, Op.cit. p242
158) Newman, Op.cit, p113
159) Bonito Oliva, Achille. Trans-Avantgarde International. 1982 Stampato in Italia. English translation Gast, Dwight and Jones Gwen. pp12-54
(160) Sayre, Op cit. p23
(161) Vidler, Anthony. The architectural uncanny: essays in the modern unhomely Massachusetts Institute of Technology 1992, p3
(162) Vidler, Op.cit. p12
(163) Walsh, Brian. *Derrida and the Messiah: The Spiritual Face of Post-modernity, http://www.thewychefamily.com/beliefs/derridaandmessiah.html*
(164) Derrida, Jacques Chapter 1 "Faith and Knowledge: The Two Sources of "Religion" at the Limits of Reason Alone" 1996 *Acts of Religion.* New York: Routledge, 2002. pp40-102
(165) Derrida, Op. cit. p55
(166) Derrida, Op. Cit. p56
(167) Walsh, Op.cit,
(168) Taylor, Victor E. Para/Inquiry: Postmodern Religion and Culture Routledge 2000. pp109-111
(169) Start, Rodney *Bringing Theory Back In,*1997 in Young, Lawrence A. (ed) "Rational Choice Theory and Religion", New York and London: Routledge 1997 in Woodhead & Heelas, op. cit. pp462-463
(170) Moore, Lawrence. R. *Selling God : American Religion in the Marketplace of Culture.* Oxford University Press 1994. pp270-3
(171) Pavis, op. cit. p4
(172) Pavis, op. cit. p11
(173) Pavis, op. cit. p17
(174) Reitmaier, Heidi. "God, Prayer and Politics: The Work of Shilpa Gupta" http://www.tate.org.uk/netart/blessedbandwidth/heidireitmaier.htm, 2003
(175) Reitmaier, Op. Cit.
(176) Elkins, Op.cit, p50 Zizek, Slavoj
(177) Reitmaier, Op. Cit.
(178) Padgett, Anthony "The Rainbow Swastika Conspiracy", Auditors of God, 2010

BIBLIOGRAPHY

Adorno, Theodor and Horkheimer, Max."The Culture Industry", Adorno, Theodor
The Culture Industry: Selected Essays on Mass Culture Rouledge 1999

Artaud, Antonin, "An Affective Athleticism" in *The Theater and its Double*, trans
Corti, Victor, Calder Publications, 1999

Artaud, Antonin, "Seraphim's Theatre" in *The Theater and its Double*, trans Corti,
Victor, Calder Publications, 1999

Artaud, Antonin, "Two Letters on Cruelty" in *The Theater and its Double*, trans Corti,
Victor, Calder Publications, 1999

Baas, Jacquelyn and Jacob, Mary Jane. "Buddha Mind In Contemporary Art",
University of California Press, 2004

Benjamin H.D. Buchloh: 'Beuys: The Twilight of the Idol,' Artforum, vol.5, no.18,
pp.35-43

Benjamin, Walter. "Dream City and Dream House, Dreams of the Future,
Anthropological Nihilism, Jung" The Arcades Project trans. Howard Eiland and
Kevin McLaughlin, London and Cambridge, Ma: Harvard University Press 1999,
K2,3,

Bois, Yve-Alain. "The Use Value of "Formless"", in Bois, Yve-Alain and Rosalind
Krauss, *Formless: A User's Guide*, New York (Zone Books), 1997,

Bonito Oliva, Achille. Trans-Avantgarde International. 1982 Stampato in Italia.
English translation Gast, Dwight and Jones Gwen.

Bradley, Fiona. Gala Dali : The Eternal Feminine in Salvador Dali: A Mythology Tate
1998,

Broadhurst, Susan *Liminal Acts: A Critical Overview of Contemporary Performance
and Theory* Cassell 2000

Buck-Morss, Susan, "Dream World of Mass Culture", The Dialectics of Seeing:
Walter Benjamin and the Arcades Project MIT Press 1991

Cecil, Paul. Even Further: The Metaphysics of Sigils in "Painful but Fabulous: The
Lives and Art of Genesis P-Orridge" Soft Skull Press 2002

Chris Burden in Fineberg, Jonathan, "Art Since 1940: Strategies of Being"
Englewood Cliffs: Prentice Hall, 1995

David Falconer, "Doctorin' the Retardis" in *Chapmanworld*

Derrida, Jacques Chapter 1 "Faith and Knowledge: The Two Sources of "Religion" at
the Limits of Reason Alone" 1996 Acts of Religion. New York: Routledge, 2002.

Dinos Chapman, "Gender is an Organic Superstition", *MAKE: The Magazine of Womens' Art,* Aug/Sept 1996

Doss, Erika. *Twentieth-Century American Art,* Oxford, 2002

Douglas Foght, London, February 27, 1995 LAAT
www.vpro.nl/data/laat/materiaal/chapman-bros-interview.shtml

Douglas Fogle, "A Scatological Aesthetics for the Tired of Seeing" in *Chapmanworld,*

Edwards, Cliff. Van Gogh and God: A Creative Spiritual Quest. Loyola University Press, 1989

Elkins, James "What Happened to Religion in Contemporary Art?"
http://www.jameselkins.com/Texts/a/religion.html, 2004

Enwezor, Okuwi, "The Black Box", *Documenta XI exhibition catalogue* (2002)

Fiat, Christopher. "The Experience of Violence in Sacrifice", *Documenta XI exhibition catalogue* (2002)

Flamiano, Dominic. "A Conversation with Jill Martin" leaflet by Techno Cosmic Mass – undated c. 2000

Fox, Matthew, A Mystical Cosmology: Toward a Postmodern Spirituality in Ray Griffin, David (Ed). "Sacred Interconnections: Postmodern Spirituality, Political Economy, and Art"

Freeland, Cynthia. Art Theory: A Very Short Introduction, Oxford University Press, 2003.

Gibson, Ian The Shameful Life of Salvador Dali Faber and Faber 1997,

Goldberg, RoseLee *Performance: Live Art since the 60's* Thames and Hudson 1998
Golding, John. Paths to the Absolute: Mondrian, Malevich, Kandinsky, Pollock, Newman, Rothko and Still, Thames & Hudson, 2000

Gomez Pena, Guillermo. *Dangerous Border Crossers: the artist talks back* Routledge 2000

Gomez-Pena, Guillermo & Sifuentes, Roberto. Temple of Confessions: Mexican Beasts and Living Santos, Powerhouse Books 1996

Goodall, Jane. Artaud and the Gnostic Drama Clarendon Press Oxford, 1994

Greenberg, Clement. Avant-Garde and Kitsch 1939, in Art in Theory 1900-1990 Harrison, Charles and Wood, Paul (Eds) Blackwell 1998

Jackson, Kevin. *Talk of the Town*, "Independent on Sunday", 1 June 2003

John Roberts, "Domestic Squabbles", in *Who's Afraid of Red, White and Blue?*

Katerina Clark and Michael Holquist, Chapter 14 – Rabelais and His World, in *Mikhael Bakhtin*, Harvard College, 1984

Kessler, Herbert L. Spiritual Seeing, University of Pennsylvania Press 2000

Koerner, Joseph Leo. Caspar David Friedrich and the subject of landscape. Reaktion 1990

Levin, Kim. "More Is More" *Village Voice*, November 27, 2002

Maia Damianovic, *Journal of Contemporary Art* 1997 **www.jca-online.com**
Mark Sladen, "The Body in Question", *Art Monthly,* no 191

Martha Schwendener, "Gagosian", *New Art Examiner*, vol 25, Dec 97/Jan 98

Mookerjee, Priya. Pathway Icons: The Wayside Art of India. Thames & Hudson 1987

Moore, Lawrence. R. *Selling God : American Religion in the Marketplace of Culture.* Oxford University Press 1994

Newman, Michael. Revising Modernism, Representing Postmodernism, in "Postmodernism: ICA documents" 1985

Padgett, Anthony "The Rainbow Swastika Conspiracy", Auditors of God, 2010

Pavis, Patrice. "Introduction: Towards a Theory of Interculturalism in Theatre?"
Pavis, Patrice. (Ed) *The Intercultural Performance Reader*. Routledge 1996

Quinn, Malcolm "The Legions of the Blind: the Philistine and Cultural Studies", Beech and Roberts (eds.) *The Philistine Controversy* Verso 2002.

Reitmaier, Heidi. "God, Prayer and Politics: The Work of Shilpa Gupta" **http://www.tate.org.uk/netart/blessedbandwidth/heidireitmaier.htm**, 2003

Roberts, John. "Domestic Squabble" in *Who's Afraid of Red, White and Blue?*

Burrows, David (ed), University of Central England, Birmingham, Article Press, 1998

Sayre, Henry. M. *The Object of Performance : the American avant-garde since 1970*. University of Chicago Press 1992

Stallabrass, Julian. *High Art Lite*, Verso 1999

Start, Rodney *Bringing Theory Back In*,1997 in Young, Lawrence A. (ed) "Rational Choice Theory and Religion", New York and London: Routledge 1997 in Woodhead & Heelas

Tate Magazine, Issue 3, http://www.tate.org.uk/magazine/issue3/michaellandy.htm
Taylor, Mark C. Disfiguring, Univ. of Chicago Press, 1992

Taylor, Mark C. Disfiguring, Univ. of Chicago Press, 1992

Taylor, Victor E. Para/Inquiry: Postmodern Religion and Culture Routledge 2000.

Tucker, Jill *Rave Spirituality* in "The Oakland Tribune" (undated)

Vidler, Anthony. The architectural uncanny: essays in the modern unhomely
Massachusetts Institute of Technology 1992

Walsh, Brian. *Derrida and the Messiah: The Spiritual Face of Post-modernity,*
http://www.thewychefamily.com/beliefs/derridaandmessiah.html

Ward, Glen. Postmodernism, Hodder Headline Limited, 2003

Whitehead, Jayson. *The Reverend Billy Wants You to Stop Shopping* in "Oldspeak",
the Rutherford Institute's Journal, **http://www.rutherford.org/articles/oldspeak-revbilly.asp**

Wilson, Julie. *As It Is* in "Painful but Fabulous: The Lives and Art of Genesis P-Orridge" Soft Skull Press 2002

Woodhead, Linda and Heelas, Paul (Ed). *Religion in Modern Times*, Blackwell 2000

www.guggenheim.org/exhibitions/warhol/warhol bottom index.html

www.palestinefacts.org/pf early palestine name origin.php

www.technocosmicmass.org/pages/about friends/about friends.html

INDEX

Zoroaster/Zoroastrianism 10, 21-4, 29-30, 34, 36, 52,
Zurvan (Zoroastrian) 22, 29, 36, 156-7,

THEORISTS

Adorno, Theodor 59-60,
Bakhtin, Mikhael 67, 91,
Bataille, Georges 68, 91, 93-4, 100-1, 111,
Baudrillard, Jean 87-8, 122,
Benjamin, Walter 59-60, 72, 74,
Blavatsky, Helena Petrovna 54-5,
Broadhurst, Susan 92,
Darwin, Charles 58, 107,
Debord, Guy 59, 73,
Derrida, Jacques 70-1, 88, 90-1, 131-2,
Einstein, Albert 58,
Elkins, James 47, 142,
Enwezor, Okuwi 99, 103, 126,
Freud, Sigmund 18, 25-6, 58, 63, 130, 156-7,
Fried, Michael 74,
Greenberg, Clement 59, 64,
Hegel, G.W.F. 50, 53-6, 78, 102, 133,
Horkheimer, Max 59-60,
Jameson, Frederick 129,
Jung, Carl 25-6, 63, 74, 140,
Kant, Immanuel 49, 65, 110, 144,
Kristeva, Julia 91,
Lacan, Jacques 89,
Levi-Strauss, Claude 89,
Luther, Martin 32,
Lyotard, Jean-Francois 85, 88, 111,
Marx, Karl 55-6, 58-9, 103,
McLuhan, Marshall 122,
More, Sir Thomas 99,
Newman, Michael 59, 65, 75, 86, 88, 129,
Newton, Sir Isaac 46, 48, 124,
Nietzsche, Friedrich 49, 52-3, 70, 79, 91-2,
Oliva, Bonito 129,
Schelling, F.W.J. 50, 53-4, 77, 98, 133,
Sontag, Susan 70,
Taylor, Marc C. 49, 54, 86, 91, 143
Taylor, Victor E. 132,

GENERAL ART

Abstract 32, 39, 43-6, 51-65, 68, 74-6, 78-81, 87, 96-8, 115, 118, 124, 130, 144, 146, 158-9,
Aesthetic 39, 43, 46-7, 49, 51, 53, 65, 67, 69, 75, 79, 92, 111, 118, 133, 144, 147, 160,
Architecture 33-4, 39-40, 121, 141,

ARTISTS

GENERAL